THE CANADIAN HEAVYWEIGHT TITLE
THE COMPLETE HISTORY 1978-1984

For all of the Maple Leaf Wrestling fans.
This is ours.

MapleLeafWrestling.com presents

THE CANADIAN HEAVYWEIGHT TITLE
THE COMPLETE HISTORY 1978-1984

by Andrew Calvert

Copyright © 2019 by Andrew Calvert. All Rights Reserved. All content by Andrew Calvert.

Layout and design by Dick Bourne at the Mid-Atlantic Gateway.

No part of this book may be reproduced or transmitted in any form or by any means, electronic or mechanical, including photocopying, recording, or by any information storage or retrieval system without permission in writing from the author. Any unauthorized use of the material within, including text, graphics, design concepts, and photographs, without specific written consent from the author will constitute infringement of copyright.

TOR.KDP.1.6.BW.191004

Independently Published by
MapleLeafWrestling.com

THE MID-ATLANTIC GATEWAY BOOK STORE
Proud to have "The Canadian Heavyweight Title" part of the Gateway family of books.
bookstore.midatlanticgateway.com

ACKNOWLEDGMENTS

Special Thanks to Roger Baker, Griff Henderson, Chris Kovachis, and Gary Will for their help with this project and for their contributions to mapleleafwrestling.com

Special thank you to Dick Bourne for his suggestion to focus on the Canadian Heavyweight Title, and of course for his great skills in designing and layout. His assistance with info, Mid-Atlantic history, photos, and editing were an invaluable help. I have always loved the look and content of the Mid-Atlantic Gateway site and of Dick's own books, and feel very proud to have that look for this book.

Thanks to a 'wishes to remain anonymous' source for much of the info contained in the epilogue.

The Canadian Title history lineage originally presented at Gary Will's "Toronto Wrestling History."

Photo thanks to Roger Baker, Dick Bourne, Jackie Crockett, Griff Henderson, Chris Kovachis, Pete Lederberg, and Chris Shwisher. Complete photo credits can be found at the back of the book.

Thanks to Ron Hutchison.

Thanks to all of the many contributors and friends of mapleleafwrestling.com over the years.

MapleLeafWrestling.com

Take a walk through the history of wrestling in Toronto at www.mapleleafwrestling.com.

Follow us us on Twitter at @mapleleafwrest1

Stranglehold
IS ANDRE THE ONE TO STOP RODDY PIPER ???
Stranglehold
"This Is It Mr. Piper— I'm Takin' That Belt From You Tonight!"
PLUS MANY OTHER EXCITING MATCHES ON TONIGHT'S CARD!!!
Stranglehold
"THE HAMMER" GREG VALENTINE MEETS ROWDY RODDY PIPER
FACE TO FACE IN TONIGHT'S MAIN EVENT!!!!
Stranglehold
WORLD TITLE SHOWDOWN!! PIPER VS. FLAIR!!
Stranglehold
SNUKA & STEVENS TO MEET ONCE MORE WITH BELLOMO OFFICIATING!!!
Stranglehold
THE GREAT KABUKI TO BE LOCKED UP INSIDE A CAGE!!!!!
Stranglehold
It's The "Battle Of The Giants"! As Andre The Giant Meets Big Hulk Hogan Here Tonight!
Plus Many Other Exciting Matches On Tonight's Card!
Stranglehold
WILL HANDSOM JIMMY STILL BE T TV CHAMPIO AFTER TONIG
Stranglehold
RIC "Nature Boy" FLAIR HEADLINES THE GREATEST CARD OF 1982!!!!
Stranglehold
FLAIR & THE GIANT- A TOUGH & POPULAR TEAM OUT FOR SOME REVENGE!
Stranglehold
BLACK— JACK'S BACK!!!
Stranglehold
IT'S CAGED MAYHEM BACKLUND vs SNUKA
Stranglehold
Dusty's Back!
He Defends His Newly Won Heavyweight Crown Here Tonight!!!
Stranglehold
SARGEANT SLAUGHTER SAYS THAT HE WILL SHOW WAHOO McDANIEL WHAT MEMBERS OF THE UNITED STATES MARINE CORPS ARE MADE OF!!!
Stranglehold
RIC "NATURE BOY" DEFENDS WORLD'S T AGAINS FORMER
Stranglehold
Official N.W.A. Wrestling Program
Sunday March 21, 1982
Indian Jay Youngblood takes on the Mysterious Ninja Tonight!!!
Stranglehold
RIC "NATURE BOY" FLAIR —
REVENGE IS ON HIS MIND!!!
Stranglehold
JIMMY "SUPERFLY" SNUKA AIMING FOR REVENGE!!!
Stranglehold
ONE MAN GANG

TABLE OF CONTENTS

	Preface	10
Chapter One:	Toronto and Frank Tunney	13
	CHART: Toronto Promoters & Affiliations	19
Chapter Two:	The Origins	22
Chapter Three:	Reloaded: The New Canadian Heavyweight Title	30
Chapter Four:	The Title Belt: TWWA?	36
	CHART: Canadian Title History: 1978-1984	40
Chapter Five:	The Title Years I	47
	Dino Bravo: The Right Choice	47
	The Hammer Takes the Title	53
	Bravo Suspended	56
	Greg & Johnny: A Toronto Legacy	54
	Mid-Atlantic Connection:	60
	Frank Tunney & Jim Crockett, Sr.	
Chapter Six:	The Title Years II	62
	Dewey Robertson: Local Hero	62
	1979 Tournament Bracket	64
	Great Hossein Arab: The Iron Sheik	68
	The Venues	72
Chapter Seven:	Angelo Mosca: Bringing the Title Home	74
Chapter Eight:	The Title Years III	82
	Mr. Fuji: A Blink of an Eye	82
	John Studd: Big Man Champ	82
	50th Anniversary Show: Nov. 15, 1981	83
	Studd-Mosca Wars Continue	85
	Kiniski Returns	90
	Sgt. Slaughter: U.S. Invasion	95
	Night of Champions / Return of the Champions: The Summer of 1983	92
	Stranglehold	98
	CHART: World Title Matches in Toronto	100
Chapter Nine:	The Title Years IV	102
	1984 Tournament & Ivan Koloff	102
	1984 Tournament Bracket	103
	Angelo Mosca, Jr.	104
	The Ramp!	108
Chapter Ten:	What's Become of the Belt	112
	Keeper of the Belt	114
	Epilogue	120
	Photo Index	125

Preface

As a youngster there was barely anything more fun than going to a Pro Wrestling card. It was an alternate universe where the heroes and villains were truly larger than life.

Living in the suburbs of Toronto, it was always an adventure going downtown to Maple Leaf Gardens. You could wait out on Wood Street behind the arena and watch the wrestlers arrive. Some in cabs or other vehicles, some walking over from the Westbury Hotel down the street.

Soon Norm Kimber would walk up the ramp into the ring and announce in his inimitable tone that the card was starting. The lights would go down for the first bout and you were in another world.

Back in the late 1970s and early 1980s, it wasn't popular to be a wrestling fan. It was a small club. We would collect magazines and get the fan bulletins like the great WWWN that let us in on some of the secrets. I even did one for a time, but it wouldn't win any awards.

The crux of my wrestling fan days was during the Mid-Atlantic era here, the same time-frame that we had our own Canadian Title.

We had our hometown heroes: Dino, Dewey, Mosca, Parisi and the rest. We would often see Ric Flair, Nick Bockwinkel, Bob Backlund, Ricky Steamboat, Blackjack Mulligan, John Studd and lots of other stars from all over the wrestling world.

At the time we didn't realize how lucky we were to be able to attend Frank Tunney's shows at MLG. We had a bit of a sense of the history, but not really. We knew The Sheik came before and there was Whipper and Frank. But that was about it.

I stopped attending the big MLG shows in 1984 as other pursuits took over. The onset of Hulkamania and especially how it played out in Toronto would change my love of wrestling - but I remained a fan.

Some years later in 2002, when I finally caught up with the online world, I was just amazed at how much (real!) info there was on the wrestling that I grew up with. I shared some of my photos and contributed some stories to Kayfabe Memories and then started a basic version of what became MapleLeafWrestling.com. I even got to see and wear the iconic Canadian Heavyweight Title belt.

Now some 35+ years later with the benefit of some historical hindsight, we will take a look back and present the story of the Canadian Heavyweight Title in Toronto 1978-1984. I hope you enjoy it.

AC
Ontario, Canada

Legendary Toronto Promoter Frank Tunney

CHAPTER ONE
Toronto and Frank Tunney: 50 Years Plus

By the time the Canadian Heavyweight Title was introduced in Toronto in 1978, the promotion had seen many ups and downs since the start of weekly cards in Toronto in 1929. Ivan Mickailoff was the first promoter to gain a foothold in the city but it was Jack Corcoran and his Queensbury Athletic Club that started a legacy that would last through most of the century.

Corcoran was a prominent Toronto businessman who owned several properties including the Queensbury Hotel. He began promoting Boxing in 1922 and after Mickailoff had proven Toronto was ready for pro-wrestling, he tried it himself in 1930. It was a slow start but when he was awarded the wrestling side at the newly built Maple Leaf Gardens in 1931, it was off and running.

Corcoran hired a young business school grad named Frank Tunney from Markham to work as the office secretary and Frank soon brought his older brother John in to the fold. Despite a great beginning, Jack would see some rough times including a bribery scandal in 1934 and a near drowning in 1939. That year would also see him fall ill with pneumonia and take an extended leave from the office. When he recovered, he decided to step away from the hustle and bustle of promoting both wrestling and boxing.

He would work out a deal with Frank and John and other investors including Paul Bowser, Jack Ganson, and Jerry Monahan to take over the office. John would serve as matchmaker but when he himself caught pneumonia in late 1939 and passed away suddenly in January 1940, brother Frank would take the reins.

Frank didn't have an easy time of it either with tough times during the war years but his easygoing demeanor (as Corcoran before him) endeared him to the wrestlers and sports writers alike. An early booster was 'Wild' Bill Longson who helped keep the fans interested until a young East York native who left Toronto as Bill Potts returned from England in 1940.

Jack Corcoran

The now re-named Whipper Watson would prove to be the key to filling up Maple Leaf Gardens on a steady basis battling the evil heels, most notably Longson and Nanjo Singh.

While there had been titles defended in Toronto before (including a local World Title in 1938) the first long term homegrown title would make its appearance in 1941 when Canadian champion Earl McCready and Watson would battle over the new British Empire Title. Watson would go on to hold that title on and off into the 1960s.

While other territories including Stampede (Calgary) and NWA All Star (Vancouver) would have a Canadian Title as their main prize, Toronto would stay with the British Empire Title. Even nearby in Windsor, ON, the Barnett-Doyle-Robertson promotion had a Canadian champion in the early 1960s held most notably by both Bobo Brazil & Gene Kiniski.

In 1962 Johnny Valentine came into Toronto billed as the U.S. champion. It has since become known as the Toronto U.S. Title and would be fought over in name right into the late 1970s. The Sheik took hold in 1969 with his Detroit based version which would see a different lineage (and belts) compared to his home base South of the border. He would defend in Toronto until wrestling his last bout for Tunney in summer 1977.

L-R: Athol Layton, Frank Tunney, Jerry Hiff (1966)

Both the NWA Title (1949-1984) and the WWWF/WWF Title (1964-1982 in the NWA era) were also defended here regularly. The city would see almost 200 appearances from the champs of the day including four NWA Title changes and the 1979 unification bout between WWF champion Bob Backlund and AWA champion Nick Bockwinkel.

There were also homegrown tag titles over the years. The Canadian Open Tag Titles 1952-1961 (represented by a trophy) and the International Tag Titles 1961-1977 that were abandoned when the Sheik era ended.

Frank with author/broadcaster Barry Lloyd Penhale in Tunney's office. (1957)

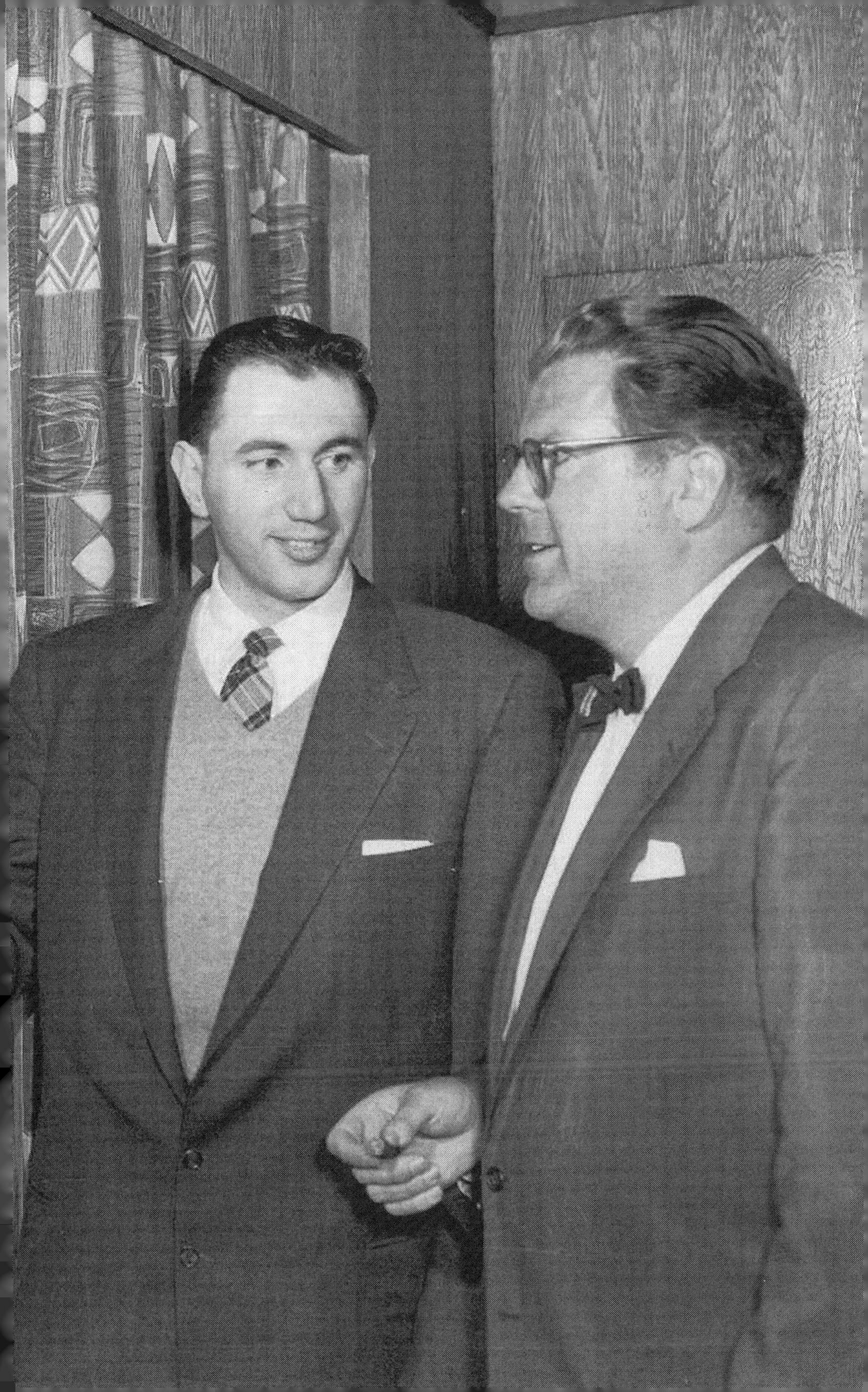

With The Sheik's departure, Tunney would work with Verne Gagne's AWA who sent in their top stars for cards running until October 1978. The new affiliation that would take place in late 1978 with Jim Crockett Promotions' Mid-Atlantic Wrestling would change the Toronto wrestling scene forever.

Frank with NWA Champion Gene Kiniski signing to meet The Sheik (1969)

An integral part of that history is the Canadian Heavyweight Title held by the top singles wrestler in the Toronto territory from 1978-1984. In this book we will look at the history of the title, the wrestlers who won it, the actual belt, and a salute to one of the greatest wrestling scenes in the world. ◆

TORONTO PROMOTERS & AFFILIATIONS

PROMOTER	TIME FRAME	PROMOTER/TERRITORIAL AFFILIATIONS
IVAN MICKAILOFF	1929 - 1938	Affiliations with Northeast U.S. Promoters Paul Bowser (Boston) & Toots Mondt (New York)
JACK CORCORAN	1930 - 1939	Affiliation with promoter Toots Mondt
FRANK TUNNEY JOHN TUNNEY	1939 - 1983 1939 - 1940	NWA DETROIT - The Sheik (Ed Farhat) 1969 - 1977 AWA - Verne Gagne 1977 - 1978 NWA MID-ATLANTIC WRESTLING - Jim Crockett, Jr. 1978-1983
JACK TUNNEY	1983 +	NWA MID-ATLANTIC WRESTLING - Jim Crockett, Jr. 1983-1984 WORLD WRESTLING FEDERATION (WWF) Vince McMahon 1984 +

EXPORT CIGARETTES

ALL STAR WRESTLING   MARCH 19TH. 7:30 P.M.

CHAPTER TWO
The Origins

When Dino Bravo was awarded the Canadian Heavyweight Title belt in Toronto in December 1978, it was the start of a new era. He was not, however, the first Canadian champion to wrestle here. Going back to the early days of professional wrestling in Canada there were Canadian champions representing the best in the country - and several of them had wrestled in Toronto.

Before the days of company mandated champions, the title of 'Canadian champion' signified the best Canadian wrestler. He would face opponents all over Canada, the U.S. and even overseas - but could only drop the title by losing to another Canadian wrestler.

George Walker was one such amateur champion who later carried the hefty rank of Canadian Champion. The Ottawa native, who was once the Canadian Middleweight champion, would appear in Toronto as Canadian champ from 1922 to 1924.

Walker was noted in Toronto for his 1922 bout against Stanislaus Zbyszko on a card at Arena Gardens that featured the touring boxing champ Jack Dempsey. Another bout versus Zbyszko in 1924 to determine who would face the World champion Ed 'Strangler' Lewis saw Walker lose when he was injured and couldn't finish the third fall. (Can't lose the title to a non-Canadian).

While Walker had appeared in several Empire Games here and in the U.K., he was billed as having been an Olympic champion (as many did) at the 1908 summer games but doesn't appear in the medal winners.

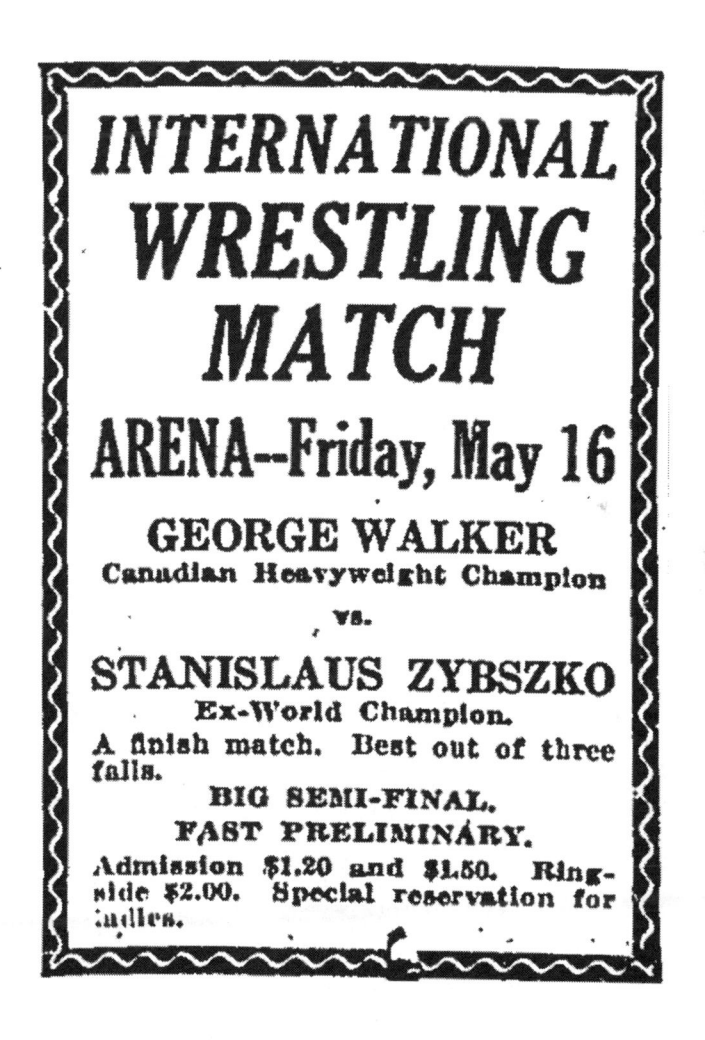

INTERNATIONAL WRESTLING MATCH

ARENA--Friday, May 16

GEORGE WALKER
Canadian Heavyweight Champion

vs.

STANISLAUS ZYBSZKO
Ex-World Champion.

A finish match. Best out of three falls.

BIG SEMI-FINAL.
FAST PRELIMINARY.

Admission $1.20 and $1.50. Ringside $2.00. Special reservation for ladies.

In 1929 as the weekly cards in Toronto commenced, Cargill (in Bruce County, ON) native 'Gentleman' Jack Taylor would appear with his cross country version of the title. He wrestled on the first Mickailoff card in May 1929, defeating Cowboy Jack Rogers in two straight falls.

CANADIAN WRESTLING CHAMPION

Jack Taylor, Canadian heavyweight wrestling champion, shown above, has been undefeated since coming to Toronto, throwing his opponents at the Saturday night wrestling show in impressive style. Next Saturday he meets Nick Volkoff, giant Hungarian, in the main bout.

Taylor also had some notable battles with Stanislaus, and brother Wladek Zbyszko, including a July 1929 bout which headed what was called 'the best night's wrestling ever shown in Toronto.' He would break his leg in a bout versus Toronto star 'Giant Killer' Stanley Stasiak, and while convalescing, it was reported that promoter Mickailoff would support him with 50$ a week.

> **INTERNATIONAL WRESTLING**
> MAPLE LEAF GARDENS
> Exhibition   THURSDAY — 8.45 P.M.
>
> **SANDOR SZABO**
> HUNGARIAN CHAMPION, VS.
>
> **EARL McCREADY**
> CANADIAN CHAMPION
> BEST TWO OUT OF THREE FALLS
>
> Semi-final—Al Getzewich vs. Jack Washburn
>
> Tickets at Moodey's, King Edward, Nicholas' and Maple Leaf Gardens—
> 60c to $2.20, tax included. Ladies 25c.
>
> AUSPICES SHAMROCK CLUB

Earl McCready, a 26 year old from a farm near Lansdowne, ON, was next in May 1931. An NCAA, Empire Games, and Olympics veteran, he was at that time known as the greatest wrestler in the country. He would appear here for the next several years as Canadian champ.

McCready had many notable bouts in Toronto and across the province and could warrant a book of his own. He remained local during that era, owning a farm in Whitchurch-Stouffville near Vandorf. He would return in between travels of the world and was known for a time as 'The Whitchurch Farmer.' In a 1944 Stouffville news item, it proclaimed Frank Tunney as the second most well-known local name in pro wrestling, next to McCready.

As the professional game grew in Canada, McCready and others would defend the title of Canadian champion in different cities across Canada, sometimes exclusively, others recognized nationally. In 1938, Quebec based star Yvon Robert would bring his version here.

Robert was Quebec's answer to Whipper Watson. He and Whipper were close in age and while Robert debuted (in Canada as a pro) a few years prior to Watson, their careers would somewhat parallel. Robert would also hold our version of the World Title (1938) and he and Whipper would have some memorable contests in 1943 over Whipper's British Empire Title. The two would team up years later in a dream team of the day as Robert was winding down his career, holding our Canadian Open Tag Titles (1953).

The Canadian Championship would return with McCready again in 1941 and he would face new star Watson. There was a disputed match with McCready winning the next one to resolve it officially. He was scheduled to meet the Quebec recognized Robert in a battle between title claimants but Robert didn't show and the title was dropped from the local cards.

The last appearance of a 'Canadian championship' (on the big circuit anyway; both Les Lyman and Red Garner featured Canadian championships on their Toronto area cards in the 1950s) prior to the return in 1978 was in 1954 when Al 'Murder' Mills, the champ in Calgary at the time, was billed as champ for one bout. Calgary had a strong Canadian Title at the time held by Kiniski, Don Leo Jonathon, Killer Kowalski, and others.

Into the boom of the 1950s, the main local prize remained the British Empire Title. It was born from the Canadian Title days in 1941 (you had to be from a member of the British Empire to win it) and symbolized a new Canadian championship. The title mostly belonged to Watson, who would hold it nine different times from 1941-1967. Long-time wrestler and Tunney associate John Katan, the 'Strongman from Palermo', who would go on to promote in Hamilton for many years, had held it. So did Nanjo Singh, Whipper's arch enemy in the early days, and others including Robert, Kiniski, Fred Atkins, and Pat O'Connor.

In the 1950s, as TV took hold and the Toronto stars became national stars, the Empire title was defended across the country. Watson and Kiniski were feuding from coast to coast and would trade the title several times, including bouts in Edmonton and Vancouver. Watson would always bring the title home from those trips where it was sometimes referred to as the Canadian Empire Title. Gene would defeat Whipper

THE CANADIAN HEAVYWEIGHT TITLE

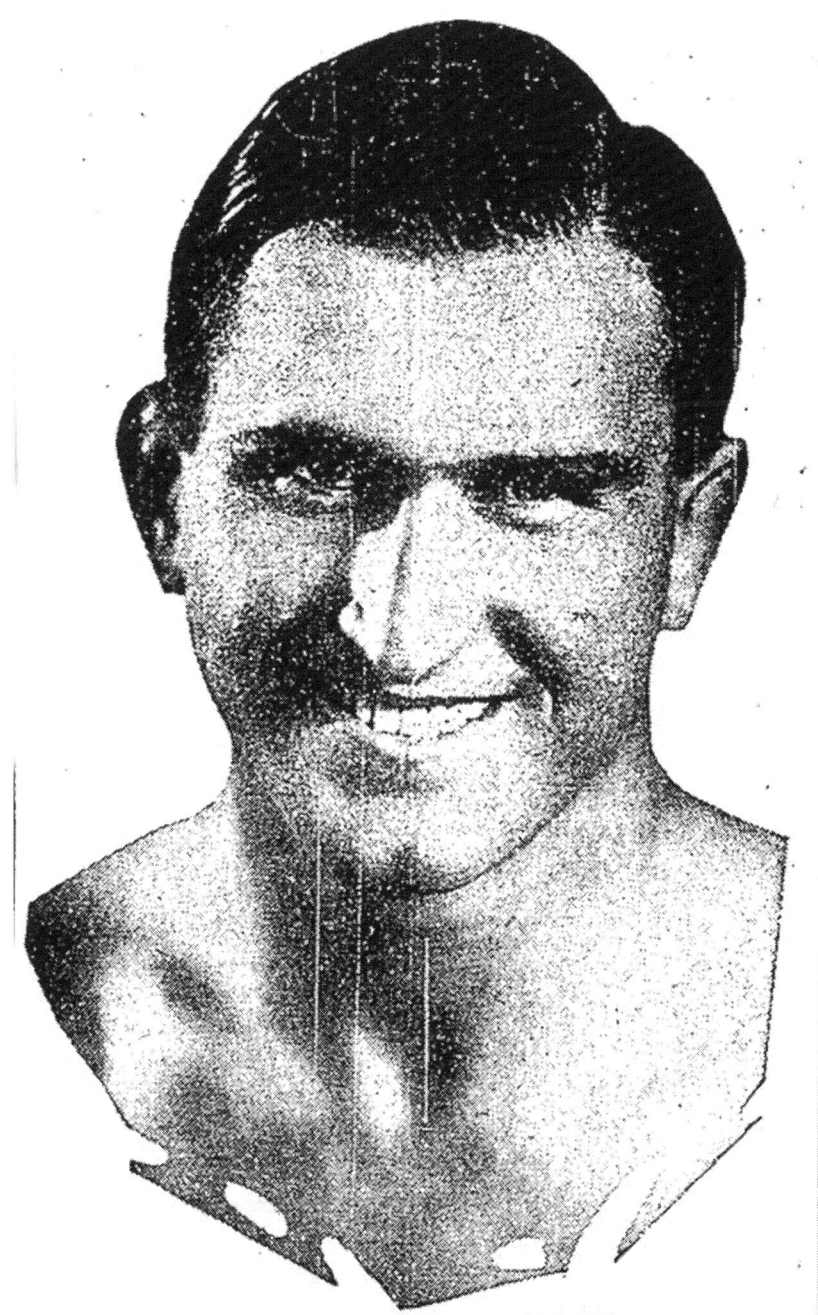

HE'S CANADA'S BEST WRESTLER
Earl McCready, Canadian heavyweight wrestling champion, had a brilliant career as an amateur and has enjoyed similar success since turning professional. Following victories over many outstanding grapplers, he will take part in one of the most important matches he has yet had when he wrestles Henri Deglane of France, former heavyweight champion of the world, at the Queensbury Club show at the Maple Leaf Gardens to-morrow evening.

BRITISH EMPIRE WRESTLING CHAMPIONSHIP

EMPIRE TITLE!

WHIPPER WATSON
Champion

vs.

LORD ATHOL LAYTON
Challenger

By Popular Request — Midgets Return

Farmer Pete & Sonny Boy Cassidy
vs.
Sky Low Low & Pancho The Bull

— also —
RAY VILLMER vs. ROBERTO PICO
JIM WRIGHT vs. WEE WILLIE DAVIS
LOU BRITTON vs. LEE HENNING

MAPLE LEAF GARDENS
TONIGHT — 8.45

here too and, though he didn't know it yet, Kiniski would have a part in the new Canadian championship 20 years later.

With the arrival of Johnny Valentine and his U.S. Title in Toronto in 1962, and the emergence of The Sheik in 1969, the U.S. Title would become the main championship in Toronto through 1977.

After they dropped the British Empire Title in 1967, the natural progression may have been a long awaited homegrown title. However, there was no way The Sheik was sharing the spotlight, so his U.S. title prevailed. Once Tunney and The Sheik parted in summer 1977, the stage was set to see a new title appear on the horizon. ◆

CHAPTER THREE
Reloaded: The New Canadian Heavyweight Title

In 1978, with attendance at its lowest levels since the late 1960s, Frank Tunney entered into an agreement with Jim Crockett, Jr. (Jim Crockett Promotions, Inc.) and George Scott (as 410430 Ontario Ltd). The three created a new entity called Frank Tunney Sports Promotions Inc. Jim Crockett, Jr. had taken over from his father Jim Sr. and the Mid-Atlantic area was on fire by the late 1970s featuring young upstarts Ric Flair, Ricky Steamboat, Jay Youngblood, and veterans including the Anderson brothers and Wahoo McDaniel.

While the agreement between Tunney, Scott, and Crockett didn't get legalized until October 1980, the stars of Mid-Atlantic championship wrestling would make their first appearance in October 1978. Right from the start, Flair and Steamboat in particular would bring the fans back in droves to Maple Leaf Gardens.

The Mid-Atlantic area had two major singles champs at the time. The Mid-Atlantic Heavyweight Title and the U.S. Title. The U.S. title would blend in seamlessly to the long lineage in Toronto dating back to Johnny Valentine in 1962. At the time of the first card to feature the Mid-Atlantic stars, Flair held the U.S. title and was embroiled in a wild feud with Steamboat. They would take over the cards with their exciting battles over the title.

Also on that first card was the Montreal based Dino Bravo. Bravo had adopted his ring name from a Toronto star of the early 1960s and was a regular on the Crockett circuit at the time as a popular babyface. He had also wrestled in Toronto debuting in the city in 1973.

Bravo would face Ken Patera and then team up with WWWF champ Bob Backlund on the next card to face AWA Tag champs Pat Patterson and Ray Stevens. Tunney was still close with Vince McMahon, Sr. and would continue to use both the WWWF/WWF and AWA champs through the association with Crockett, Jr. and Scott. Bravo would also be seen on the Maple Leaf TV show both on his own and teaming with Steamboat.

The third card featuring the Mid-Atlantic stars would take place on December 17 and would see Steamboat beat Flair to take the U.S. Title in the main event. In the semi Bravo would face Gene Kiniski for the newly created Canadian Heavyweight Title. In some reports it had been called a final of a tournament. In others, including the ad for the card it was called a bout for the 'vacant title.' This is prior to the return to the circuit shows for Tunney and there is no evidence that there had been any other bouts to determine challengers for the new title.

Gene Kiniski was years into a long association with Toronto having been one of the biggest stars in the city since his debut here

> **Ottawa approves six takeovers**
>
> OTTAWA (CP) — The government yesterday announced approval of six applications by foreign groups or individuals to establish or take over Canadian companies under the Foreign Investment Review Act.
>
> Accepted were applications by:
>
> ☐ Frank Tunney Sports Ltd. of Toronto, Jim Crockett Promotions Inc., of Charlotte, N.C., and 410430 Ontario Ltd., of Hamilton, to establish a Toronto business called Frank Tunney Sports Promotion, to stage wrestling events at Maple Gardens and, in the summer months, at other Ontario locations.

in 1956. Through his NWA Title reign in the late 1960s and into the Sheik era, he remained a regular on the Toronto scene. He had also been a Canadian champion in both Calgary and Vancouver and while staying mostly around his home base in Vancouver by 1978, he was still regarded as a top challenger in the NWA.

The night December 17, 1978 had been appointed 'Whipper Watson Appreciation Night' to recognize him for all he had done for Toronto wrestling as well as all of his charity work on behalf of disabled children. That year marked 30 years of his association with the Easter Seals. One dollar of every admission would go to a scholarship in Watson's name to help the boys who served as

First Toronto Card featuring the Mid-Atlantic Stars

each year's Easter Seals 'Timmy' (Watson would carry the child - emblematic of all disabled children - on his shoulders to kick off each year's dinners dating back to the 1950s). As an added bonus, Whipper was to present the new title belt symbolic of the Canadian championship to the winner of the Bravo-Kiniski bout.

> PHONE 363-1093
>
> ## FRANK TUNNEY SPORTS LIMITED
>
> MAPLE LEAF GARDENS
> 466 CHURCH STREET
> TORONTO 5, CANADA
>
> WHIPPER WATSON APPRECIATION NIGHT
> "*Timmy Scholarship Fund*"
>
> On Sunday night, December 17th at Maple Leaf Gardens, there will be a "WHIPPER WATSON APPRECIATION NIGHT" not only to remember his many feats in the Wrestling Ring, but his tireless efforts on behalf of the handicapped.
>
> To this end, there will be inaugurated, a "*Timmy Scholarship Fund*", which will be a Fund to help young people who have served as "*Timmy*" (representing Ontario physically handicapped children in the annual Easter Seal appeal), to obtain Post-Secondary education.
>
> To launch this "*Timmy Scholarship Fund*", One Dollar from every ticket sold for the WHIPPER WATSON APPRECIATION NIGHT, on Sunday, December 17th, will be donated to the "*Timmy Scholarship Fund*".
>
> Whipper has received many awards over the years, but this is the first time that wrestling fans will be able to say thanks in a tangible way, for the countless thrills and excitement he provided during his illustrious career.

The card also had, for the first time in many years, an autograph table set up featuring Bravo, Steamboat, Paul Jones, and Jimmy Snuka signing and handing out free (yes free!) photos of themselves.

Special guest Watson and Bravo's challenger Kiniski had a long history together dating back to Kiniski's early days in Toronto. At Whipper's introduction, Kiniski blew up and berated the then 62 year old Watson in what was the in-ring final chapter to their long feud.

Dino Bravo & Whipper Watson, Dec. 17, 1978

> **Special events**
>
> **Whipper Watson Appreciation Night:** To remember his many feats in the wrestling ring and his tireless efforts on behalf of the handicapped, Dec. 17 at 7:30 p.m. has been appointed Whipper Watson Appreciation Night at Maple Leaf Gardens in which $1 from every ticket sold will be donated to the Timmy Scholarship Fund, a fund to help young people who have served as Timmy, to obtain post-secondary education. Wrestling promoter Frank Tunney has signed a wrestling card befitting the evening featuring the United States title match, the Canadian heavyweight crown and the World tag team title match. Maple Leaf Gardens. Tickets $3 to $6. 363-1093.

The bout in which Bravo was perceived to be the underdog saw Bravo and Kiniski taking turns throwing each other out of the ring. Kiniski got in some of his big kicks and stomps with Bravo countering with a high flying head scissors and a faster pace which took its toll on Kiniski.

Bravo would earn the pin at 14:58 of the bout and Whipper would present the title belt to the new champ. The new Canadian Heavyweight Title representing the best in Toronto would go on to be defended here over the next 6 years., the final years with Toronto as an NWA stronghold. ◆

CHAPTER FOUR
THE TITLE BELT: TWWA?

The actual title belt that was presented to Bravo was a bit of an enigma. It proudly declared 'TWWA Heavyweight Wrestling Champion'. The belt, a cast design, was made by noted Toronto based belt maker and artist Alex Mulko. Mulko had started wrestling in Toronto in 1961 as Nikita Kalmikoff alongside wrestling 'brother' and long-time Toronto regular Ivan Kalmikoff.

He would also wrestle across North America and Worldwide by other names, most notably Nikita Mulkovich. In his later wrestling days he had turned to managing, including guiding The Rugged Russians (Pedro Godoy & Juan Sebastian) a masked team in the WWWF.

Originally from the Ukraine, Mulko spoke six languages and traveled the world but had settled in Toronto. He specialized in sculptures, paintings, and other artistic endeavours. He was also an avid violin collector and had once been a foundry engineer making submarine and airplane molds that were used in mass production.

Oil paintings were his milieu and he was said to have sold many of them, mostly portraits, to notables including the Governor of Oklahoma. Here long time Tunney pal and Toronto stalwart 'Tiger' Tommy Nelson had a Mulko portrait of himself done when he was in his 70's (back in the early 1970's).

He also made custom belt buckles for fellow wrestlers in the early 1960's including one for promoter Tunney. He would turn to wrestling title belts in the late 1960's and produced many of the belts used around the territories in the 1970's.

He also created our own International Tag Title belts, several WWWF Championship belts and tag belts, and belts for the East Coast Title, several U.S. Titles, the Texas Heavyweight Title, Florida Tag, and many more. If it had that oval plate cast design with side plates it was likely a Mulko creation.

ALEX MULKO, aka NIKITA MULKOVICH

In correspondence to his family in the 1970's, Mulko explained the belts sold for around 500$ and that he had made about 50 belts.

For years we had discussed the lettering of TWWA on the title belt. A good assumption was that it stood for Toronto Wide/World Wrestling Association/Alliance. That designation had never been used here publicly at least. Since 1977 the area had been known simply as Maple Leaf Wrestling.

TWWA Crew (L-R): Bulldog Brower, Hans Schmidt, Waldo Von Erich, Lou Thesz, Stan Kowalski, Fred Atkins, and Danny Hodge

The TWWA, as we learned years later, actually stood for the Trans World Wrestling Association.

As it turns out the TWWA had a strong connection to Toronto wrestling. In 1969 Danny Hodge and Lou Thesz attempted to run a new promotion in Japan. In some notes Tunney was said to be one of the initial backers for the start up.

In addition to Thesz, who had both won and lost the NWA Title in Toronto, they enlisted well-known local stars Fred Atkins, Bulldog Brower, and Waldo Von Erich.

CANADIAN TITLE HISTORY
OCTOBER 1978 - JUNE 1984
(All matches at Toronto's Maple Leaf Gardens except where noted.)

DATE	CHAMPION	CHALLENGER	NOTE
78/12/17	DINO BRAVO	GENE KINISKI	Bout to name the new Canadian Heavyweight Champion.
79/04/08	GREG VALENTINE	DINO BRAVO	
79/06/03	DINO BRAVO [2]	GREG VALENTINE	
79/09	TITLE VACATED		Dino Bravo leaves the area.
79/09/09	DEWEY ROBERTSON	GREG VALENTINE	Robertson defeats Valentine in the finals of tournament.
80/05/25	GREAT HOSSEIN ARAB (THE IRON SHEIK)	DEWEY ROBERTSON	
80/07/20	ANGELO MOSCA	GREAT HOSSEIN ARAB (THE IRON SHEIK)	
80/08/10	GREAT HOSSEIN ARAB (THE IRON SHEIK) [2]	ANGELO MOSCA	
80/12/28	ANGELO MOSCA [2]	GREAT HOSSEIN ARAB (THE IRON SHEIK)	
81/07/12	MR. FUJI	ANGELO MOSCA	
81/07/26	ANGELO MOSCA [3]	MR. FUJI	
81/09/20	JOHN STUDD	ANGELO MOSCA	
82/01/17	ANGELO MOSCA [4]	JOHN STUDD	
83/07/24	SGT. SLAUGHTER	ANGELO MOSCA	Match takes place at Toronto's Exhibition Stadium.
84/01/22	ANGELO MOSCA [5]	SGT. SLAUGHTER	
84/04	TITLE VACATED		Angelo Mosca said to be injured.
84/04/29	IVAN KOLOFF	BRIAN ADIDAS	Koloff defeats Adidas in the finals of a tournament.
84/06/10	ANGELO MOSCA, JR.	IVAN KOLOFF	
84/06	TITLE RETIRED		Promoter Jack Tunney aligns with the World Wrestling Federation.

Atkins served 40 years on the local scene here as a wrestler, trainer, manager, and referee. Von Erich was once Wally Seiber from Holland Landing, Ontario, just North of Toronto, while Brower was a top heel - and Toronto based - during the 1960's. Hans Schmidt and Stan Kowalski, both familiar names in Toronto, rounded out the North American side.

Hodge and Thesz traded the championship of the TWWA back and forth in the short time the promotion was active in Japan. While that may explain the connection, the title belt Hodge and Thesz wore - was a totally different belt.

The TWWA belt to be used for the Toronto based Canadian Heavyweight Title was apparently made for the TWWA but not used. If the Tunney connection is accurate it may have now been Tunney's belt to use. Toronto now had a new homegrown championship. ◆

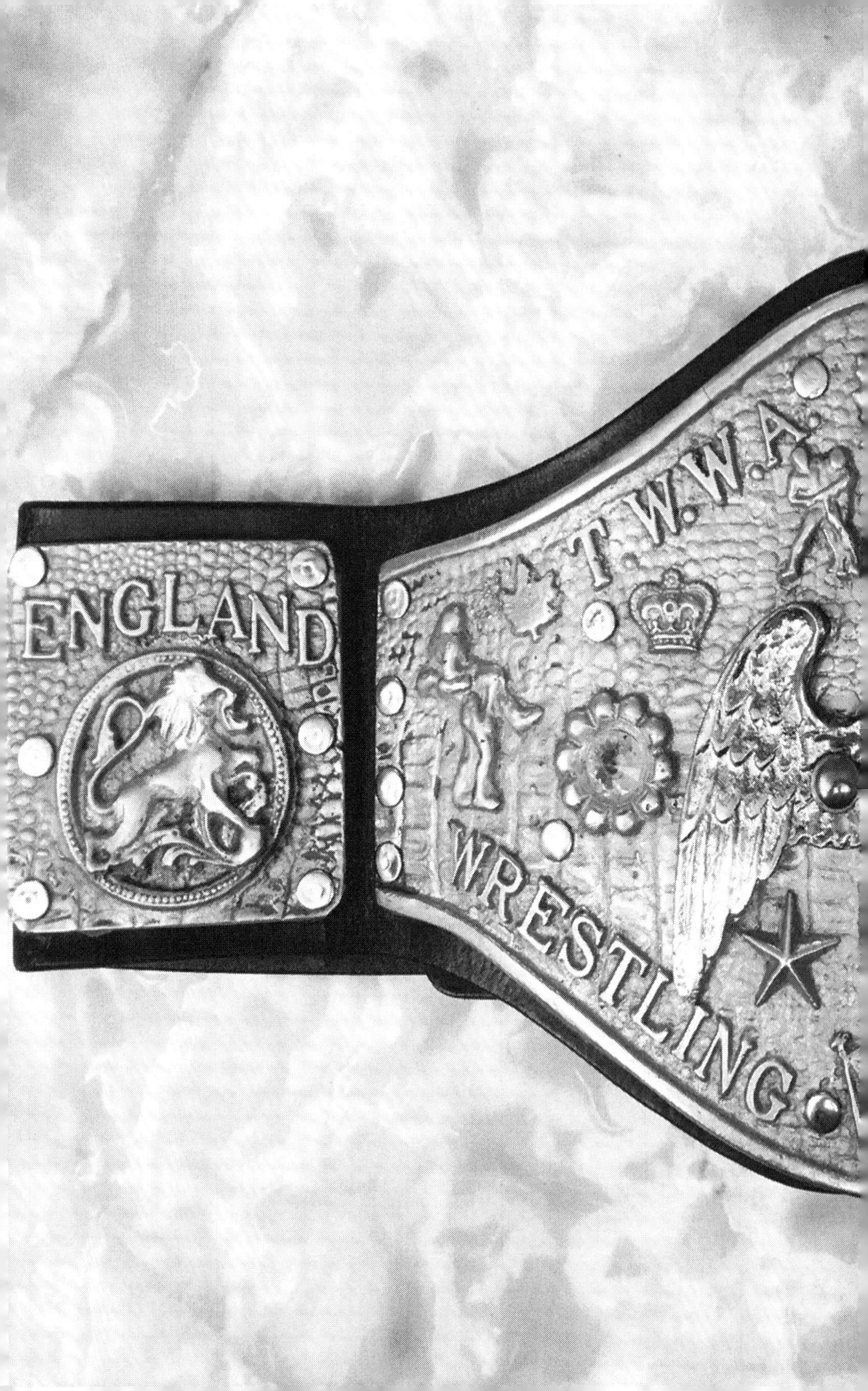
ENGLAND
T.W.W.A.
WRESTLING

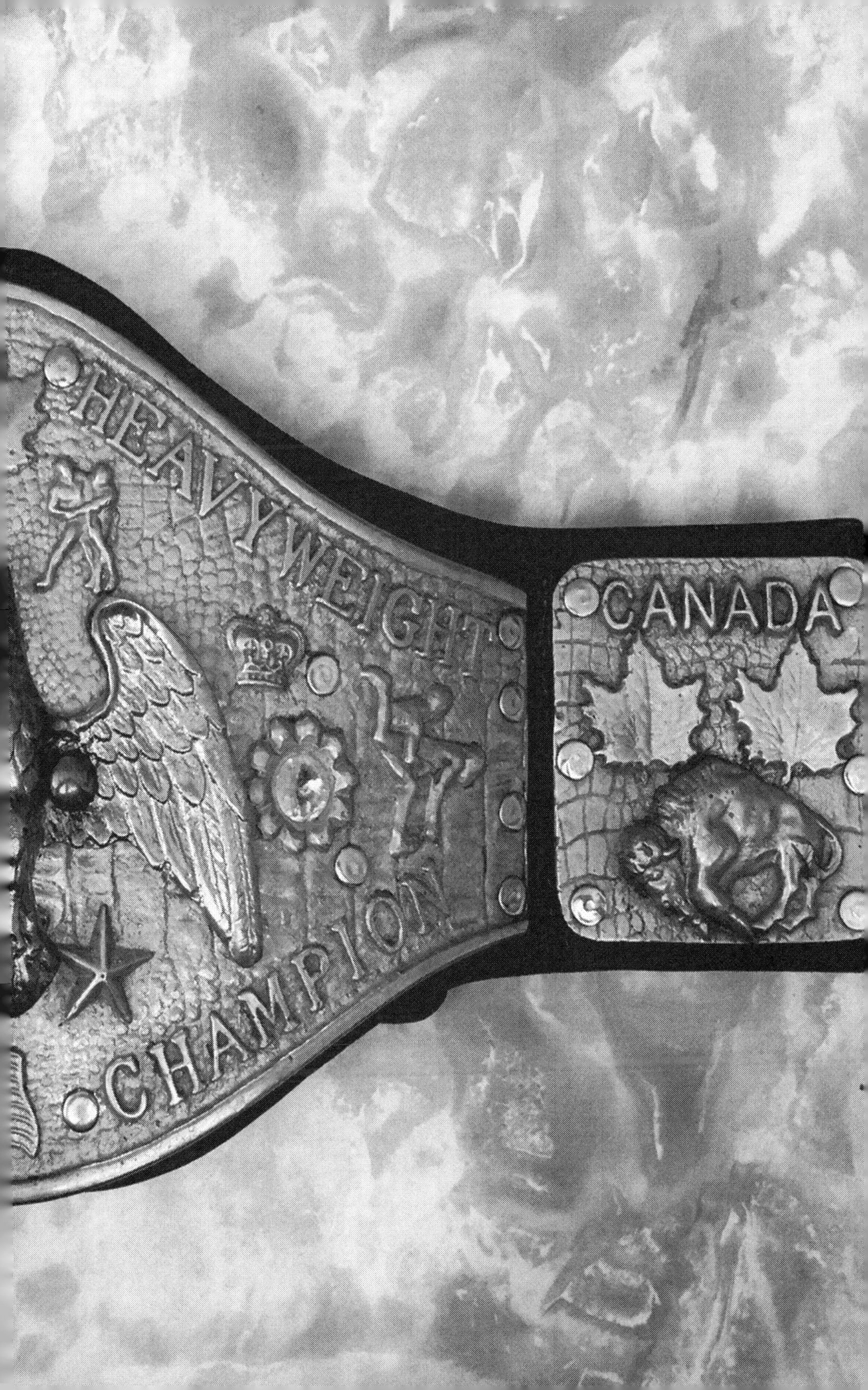
HEAVYWEIGHT
CHAMPION
CANADA

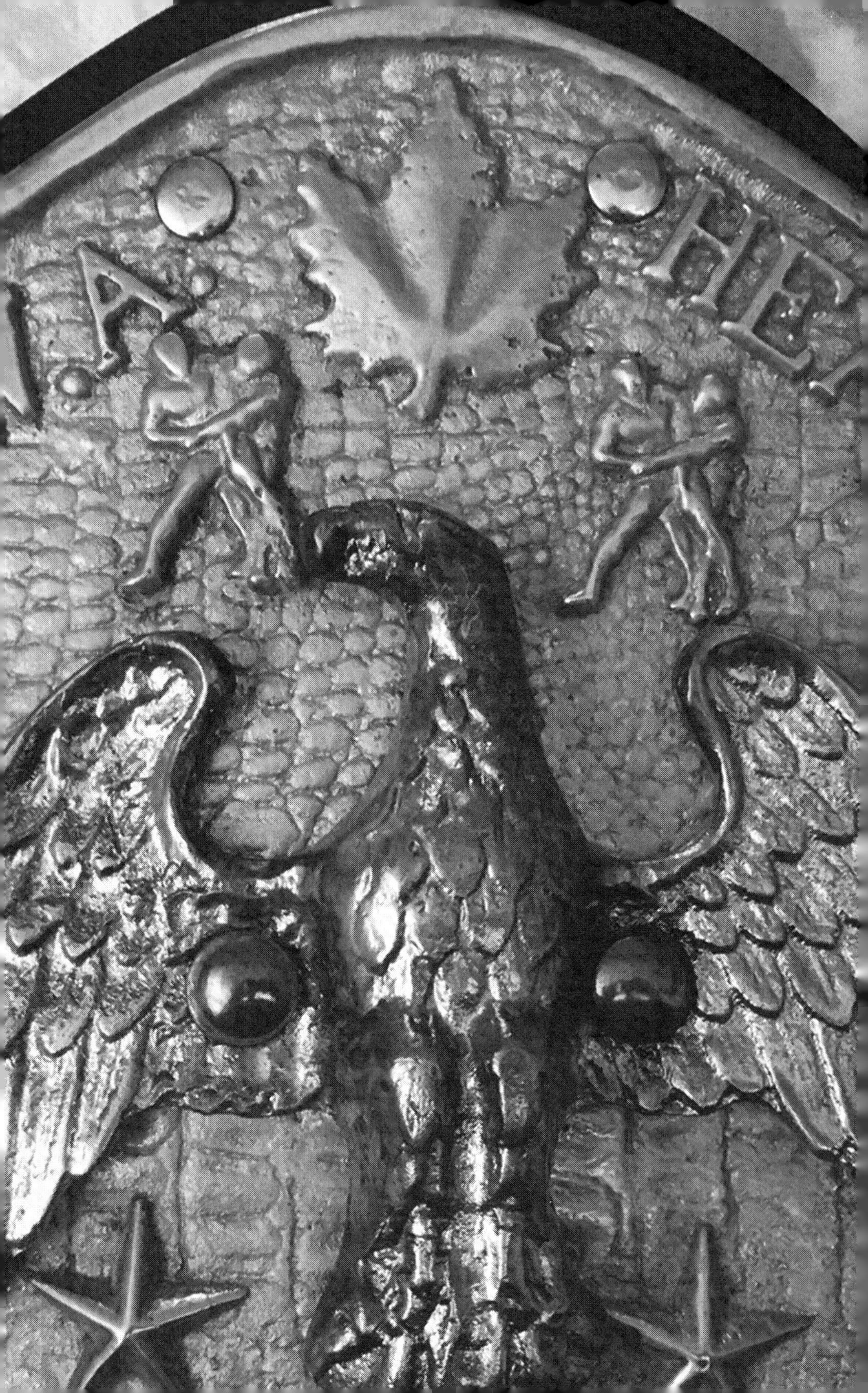

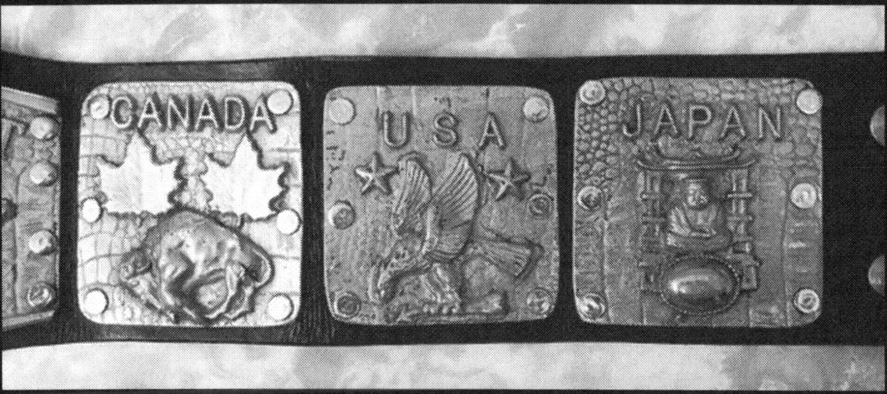
CANADA
USA
JAPAN

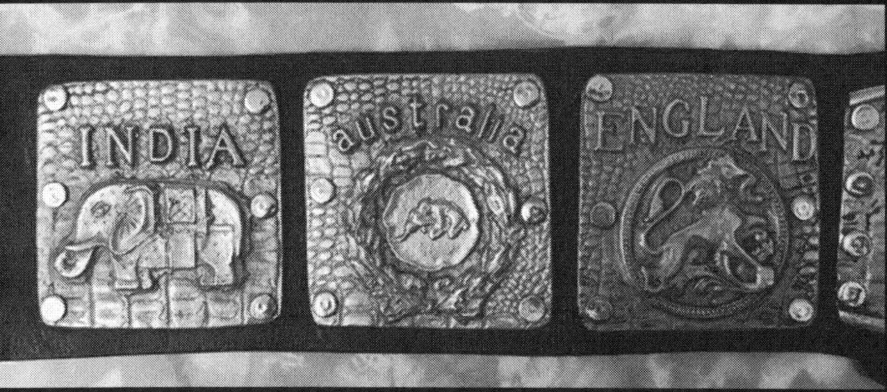
INDIA
australia
ENGLAND

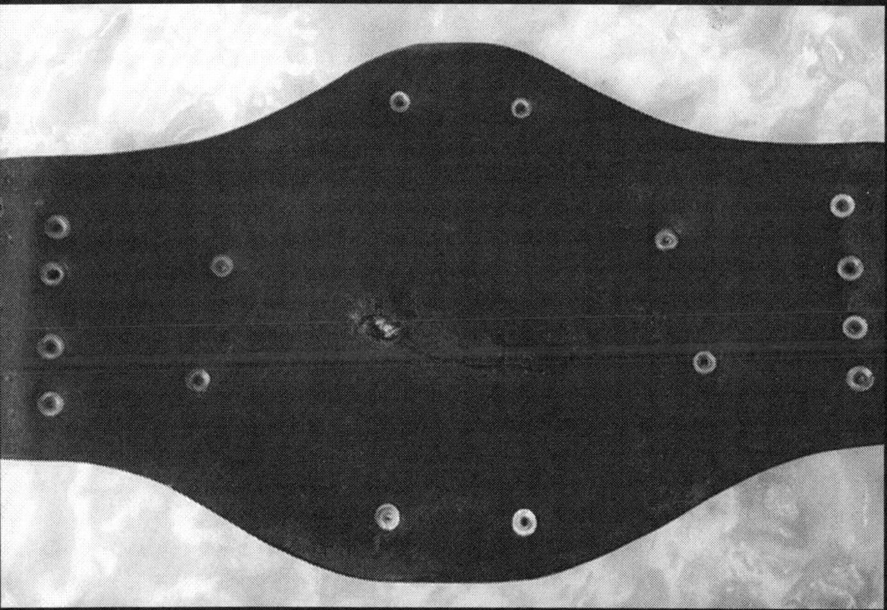

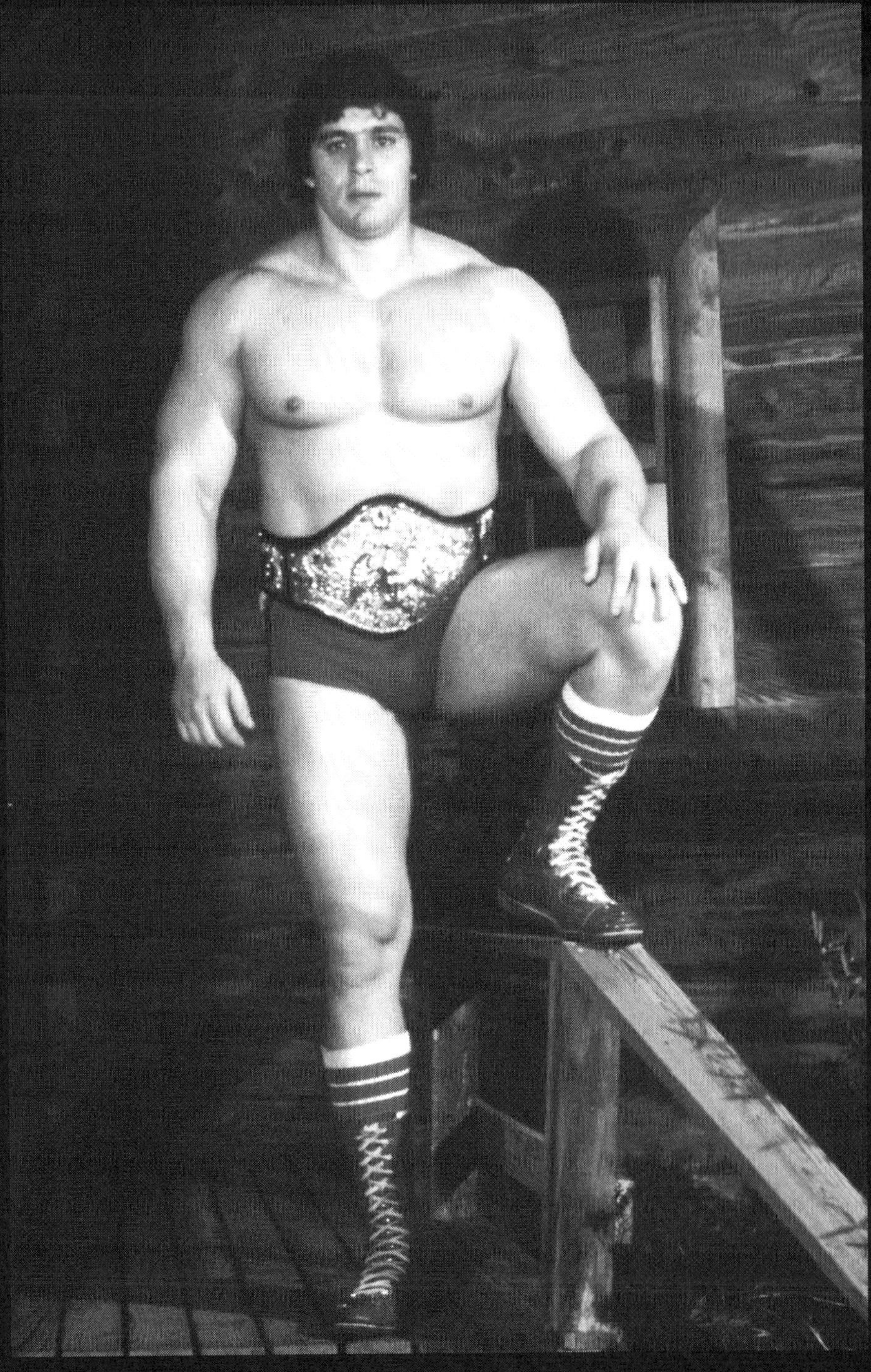

CHAPTER FIVE
The Title Years I:
Bravo • Valentine

Dino Bravo: The Right Choice

After Bravo had won the Canadian Title by beating Kiniski, he flew right out of Toronto (his new home, he had moved here in 1977) to New York City where he appeared the next night at Madison Square Garden in a 6-man tag bout with partners Domenic Denucci and Dusty Rhodes vs. Ivan Koloff, Victor Rivera, and Lumberjack Pierre.

Interestingly, regular tag partner Denucci had wrestled here as Domenic Bravo alongside the original Dino Bravo in 1961. Our Canadian champ Bravo had been a regular in the WWWF through the 1970s and he and Denucci had held the fed's tag titles earlier in 1978. He had also held the tag titles in the Mid-Atlantic area with partner Tim 'Mr. Wrestling' Woods.

Bravo would prove to be a great choice to launch the Canadian Title. He was fast, agile, and could wrestle with a variety of opponents. This was before he bulked up considerably in his later years. He was an exciting and well versed wrestler who had established himself as

Canadian Champion Dino Bravo at Maple Leaf Gardens

one of the 'young guns' alongside Flair, Steamboat, and others who were bringing pro wrestling to a new generation.

With the increase in popularity, Tunney would start to go back to a circuit around Southern Ontario. After an absence of many years, the office would again run the towns outside Toronto. The big shows at Maple Leaf Gardens were on Sundays (and an occasional Saturday) while other towns that had seen diminished wrestling over the years would see it return.

Tunney had once promoted weekly cards at the Gardens and was now running about two cards a month at MLG. Over the next few years they would return to the circuit towns including Kitchener,

Oshawa, Niagara Falls, London, Hamilton, Brantford, Guelph, Kingston, Ottawa, and even Buffalo, NY for a time. The landscape was opening back up for the local guys as well as the Mid-Atlantic stars that would often stay on for the extra shows.

Even with all of the extra shows added there was often weeks in between where our local stars including Bravo could travel outside the area. Bravo would continue his Carolinas-based feud with Greg Valentine before returning to Toronto in January 1979 to face AWA champ Nick Bockwinkel.

Bravo and Bockwinkel had met before in the AWA and their bout here did not disappoint. Only the AWA Title was on the line with Bravo winning by disqualification over the champ when Bockwinkel tossed him over the top rope to save his title. It could only be seen as a positive with our local champion being able to win (the bout, not the belt) making Bravo appear a very capable champion.

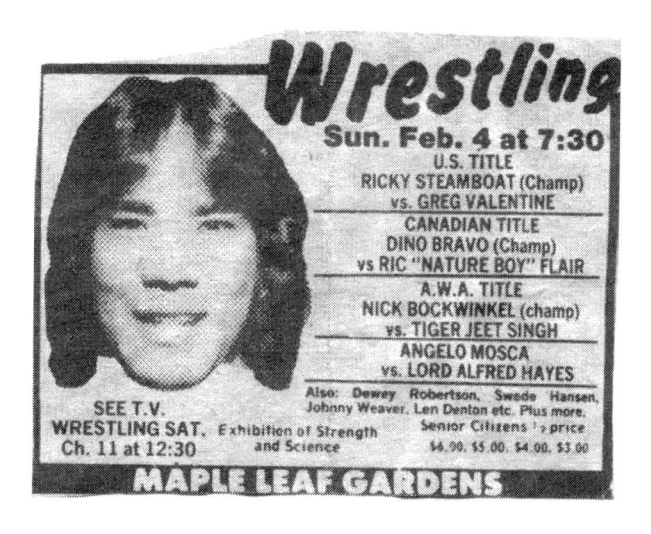

In the time between the next MLG show, Bravo would maintain a busy schedule in the U.S. battling Valentine, Flair, and Gene Anderson and tagging with Tony Atlas. He would also appear on the TV show Mid-Atlantic Championship Wrestling with the Canadian belt to battle Len/Lynn Denton (aka The Grappler). He would return to face Flair on the next MLG show in February pinning him in 19:35 to retain the title. It was a good start with wins over Bockwinkel & Flair to start his reign.

He would appear on the regular Saturday Maple Leaf show usually matched against a prelim wrestler or in a tag bout with Tiger Jeet Singh or other local stars. On the Mid-Atlantic circuit, he and Steamboat would team in a popular tag and when they returned to Toronto in March 1979, the two would face Flair and Greg Valentine. Steamboat was the U.S. champ at the time and he and Bravo would beat the short lived team of Flair & Valentine by disqualification after Flair threw Bravo over the top rope at 30:17 of the one fall bout.

Tony Atlas and Canadian Champion Dino Bravo team up in Charlotte.

On the U.S. circuit, Bravo would feud with recently turned heel Paul Jones over the NWA TV Title and continue his winning ways before returning to Toronto on March 25 to face Greg Valentine.

Known as 'The Hammer', Greg was continuing the legacy of father Johnny in Toronto. With a similar style and no-nonsense approach to his Dad, Greg would prove to be a formidable challenger for Bravo. They were well matched and equally adept at both scientific wrestling and all-out brawling.

Greg had debuted here early in his career in 1970 as 'Babyface Nelson' while father Johnny was still a regular in Toronto. With the introduction of the Mid-Atlantic stars, Greg was primed to enjoy a long relationship with Toronto that would continue into the WWF years.

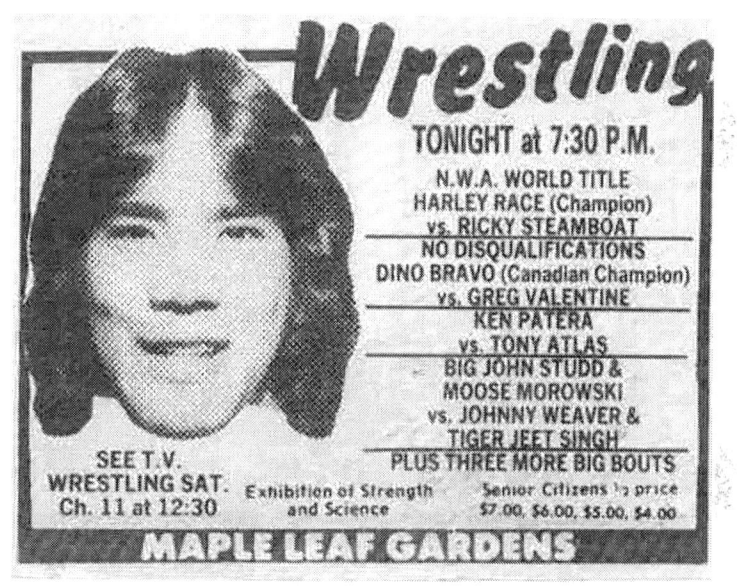

Title change: Greg Valentine defeats Dino Bravo to win the Canadian Title April 8, 1979

In their first meeting at Maple Leaf Gardens, Bravo would earn the disqualification from referee John Laing when he heaved Valentine over the top rope after 14:18 of action. Both wrestlers were bloody by the finish. This card also featured the WWF/AWA Title vs. Title bout as well as Steamboat successfully defending his U.S. Title against Flair.

The return set for two weeks later with a no-DQ stipulation ended up in a bloody bout that had them fighting outside the ring and using Norm Kimber's announcers table to batter each other. Both Bravo and Valentine were again covered in blood by the time Valentine pinned Bravo to become the next Canadian Heavyweight champion.

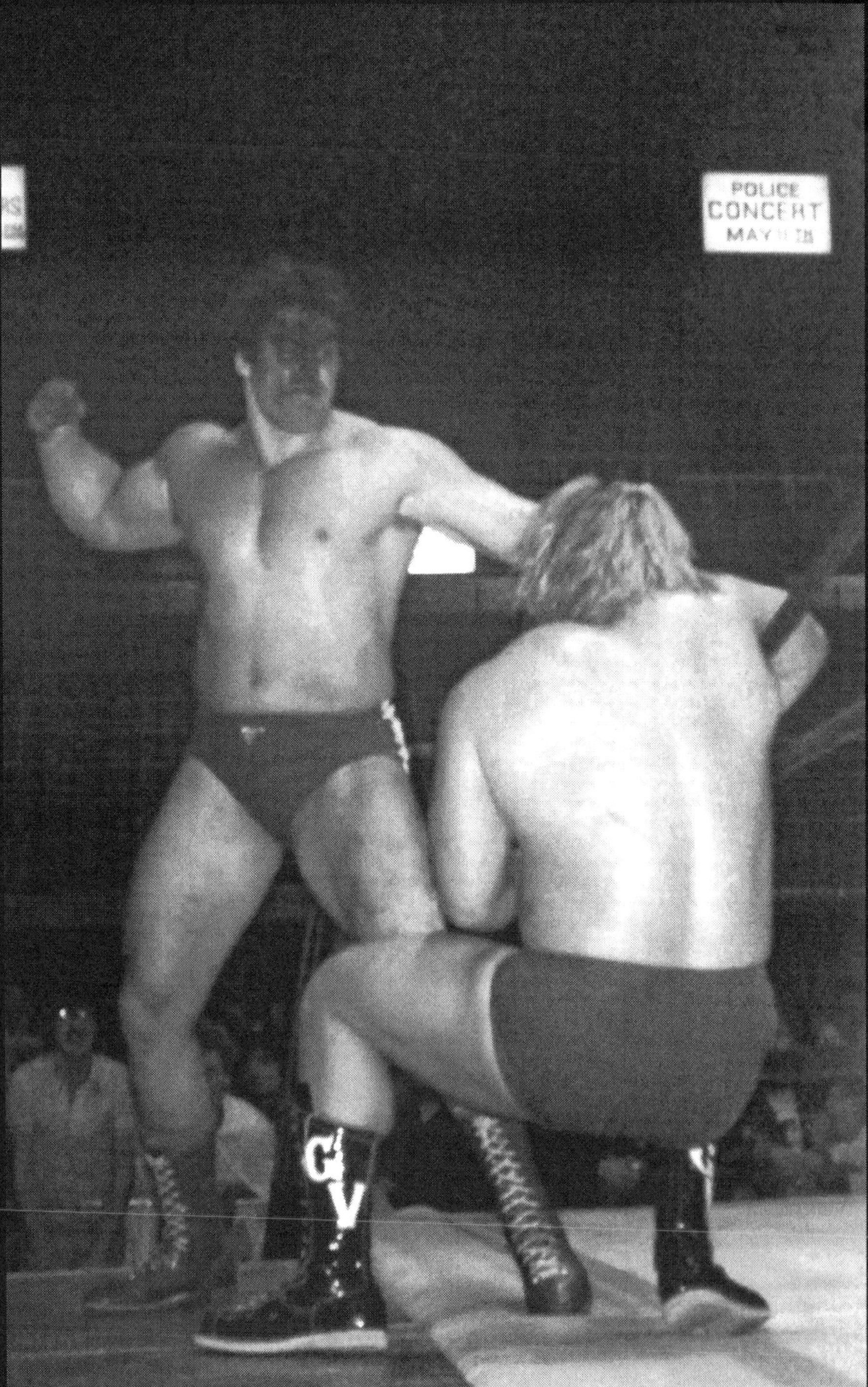
POLICE
CONCERT

The Hammer Takes The Title

New Canadian champion Greg Valentine would return for the next MLG card in May 1979 to give Bravo a re-match. Bravo would win by count-out when a frustrated Valentine took the title belt and left for the dressing room after a tough battle. He would also be seen on TV in tags teaming with Flair against Leo Burke & John Bonello, as well as Burke and 'Silent' Brian Mackney (a local deaf wrestler).

During his reign as Canadian champion, Greg Valentine was busier outside the area, working a regular schedule in the WWF proper with The Grand Wizard as his manager. He didn't officially defend the Canadian title there (as far as we know) but carried it backstage with Wizard by his side.

In the magazines of the day, they called him the number one contender to Backlund's title. He had been challenging Backlund in the Northeast for the first few months of the year and sandwiched the Bravo re-match here in between a long stretch of daily shows up and down the Northeast coast.

While he didn't have a long run with the title, Valentine would prove to be a successful champion in one way - - he was beating Backlund in many of their contests but unable to secure the belt.

In another rematch with Bravo at MLG three weeks later with Lumberjack rules (other wrestlers around the ring to keep the combatants inside), Bravo would pin Valentine after a huge backdrop and take the title back to begin his second reign.

Greg & Johnny: A Toronto Legacy

When Greg captured the Canadian Title in 1979, he was following in his father's Toronto footsteps. Large footsteps.

Johnny Valentine had debuted in Toronto in 1962 with his U.S. Title and would make the area his home away from home for the next several years. Thirteen years in fact, from 1962-1975. If we only count the NWA years in Toronto, Greg also served a little over thirteen years from 1970-1984, if you include a 1970 bout as Babyface Nelson.

Johnny would later turn fan-favorite in a feud with The Beast (Johnny Yachetti) and his manager Martino Angelo, though his ring

Johnny Valentine vs. NWA champ Gene Kiniski January 1967

style would stay the same. While in Toronto, he would also challenge for the NWA World title facing NWA champs Lou Thesz (twice, 1963, 1965), Gene Kiniski (five times, 1966-1967), Dory Funk Jr. (1973), and Jack Brisco (twice, 1973, 1974).

In 1967 he would enter into a series with new star Tiger Jeet Singh, now the U.S. champ, and his manager Fred Atkins. One bout at the

Gardens goes an hour with the re-match set for the old Maple Leaf Stadium on the Toronto lakeshore.

A bout at the end of July 1967 saw the two in a rare 90-minute time limit bout at the outdoor venue. The bout would go to an 89:27 curfew draw. The re-match a week later with two referees was set for a two hour limit to start at 9 PM (curfew of 11 PM). Singh would be disqualified to set up a return bout. They would meet in a third match with the same stipulations, as well as Tiger Jeet to lose his title if he was to lose by disqualification. This time they went the full two hours to a draw.

Valentine vs. Bravo, Maple Leaf Gardens, 1979

As the 1960s turned to the 1970s, his role would be mostly reduced working in the middle of the cards though he would see some main events again. In the upcoming years he would join the long line to face The Sheik twice during the Sheik's winning streak here (127 bouts without a loss, 1969-1974).

He and Greg would appear on the same cards a number of times when Greg returned here as Johnny Fargo in 1972. Greg (as Fargo) would team with Chris Colt while Johnny took on Man Mountain (George) Cannon on one card while another saw Greg take on Danny Hodge in Hodge's only Toronto appearance. On that card Johnny took on Chris Colt.

When Johnny faced Brisco in 1974 in what was to be his last MLG main, Greg teamed with Chris Tolos against Domenic Denucci and the now fan-favorite Beast on the undercard. Johnny's last appearance here before the tragic plane crash which ended his career was in July 1975 when he battled Tolos on the undercard of a Sheik - Stan Stasiak main.

Greg followed in his Dad's footsteps in the Mid-Atlantic area too. Greg had arrived there in September of 1976 and by the time he won the title here in mid-1979, he had carved out a successful career in several of the old-school territories.

When Greg arrived at Maple Leaf Gardens in December of 1978 with his own 'skullcrusher' elbow smash now called 'the hammer', many of the older fans remembered the tough as nails Johnny Valentine. The kid was a chip off the old block. ◆

Bravo Suspended

To begin his second reign with the Canadian Title, Bravo would go up against Ric Flair while former champ Valentine rebounded by facing WWF champ Bob Backlund the same night at MLG.

Next up for Bravo were strongman Ken Patera and his finishing move, the swinging neckbreaker. They would both end up disqualified by referee Terry Yorkston after the bout erupted into an all-out brawl. Backlund, by now a familiar sight on the Toronto cards, also returned to defend the WWF title against Flair. Having our champs and their challengers all intertwined with the big titles would continue to raise the prestige of our own Canadian Title.

The day after the MLG card, WWF champ Backlund would stay on for a rare non-Toronto appearance in Oshawa, ON. He would team with Canadian champ Bravo in an 'dream team' of sorts to take on the two challengers to their titles: Valentine and Patera, in a tag bout.

On August 6, 1979, Bravo missed a date in Winston-Salem, NC, set to team with Steamboat against World tag champs Paul Jones and Baron Von Raschke. Two weeks later Bravo and Patera were set to go again at MLG but Bravo missed the show. He was replaced by Backlund who defended his title successfully against Patera. During the card it was announced that Bravo had suffered an injury and would not be able to wrestle.

A couple of weeks later it was reported in the paper that Bravo had suffered a serious injury that would keep him out of wrestling for a year or so.

It appeared to heal fast as Bravo would soon show up on AWA cards (and the Winnipeg AWA TV show that aired here) wrestling without injury as early as September, 1979. In December the now billed as AWA Canadian champion (no belt) Bravo would again meet AWA champ Nick Bockwinkel, this time at the Winnipeg Arena.

A re-match with Bockwinkel in Winnipeg would see who else but Gene Kiniski as special referee for the bout.

Some months later, the AWA set up some shows in Ottawa, ON, in tandem with Promoter Ray Boucher who had ties to the

Injured Bravo Forced To Give Up Canadian Title

TORONTO, ONT., CANADA— Injuries have done what no man could do. They've taken the Canadian heavyweight title from Dino Bravo.

"I can't talk about it," mumbled Bravo moments after the official announcement. "I'm too upset."

WHO'S NEXT?

A one-night elimination tournament has been established to determine a new champion. Such names as Ken Patera and Rick Steamboat will participate in this grueling tourney.

Popular Dino Bravo has been forced to relinquish his Canadian title because of injuries.

Quebec scene. Bravo was still billed as Canadian champion and was scheduled to face Jerry Blackwell during their feud centered on a bodyslam challenge. Bravo missed the show (Blackwell took on Johnny War Eagle) and it was reported that he had not appeared as he was still under a suspension from the OAC - The Ontario Athletic Commission - which regulated Boxing and Wrestling within Ontario.

Dino Bravo ready for grudge match

A suspension against Canadian professional wrestling champion Dino Bravo of Montreal has been lifted, enabling him to continue his series of grudge matches with 428-pound Gerry Blackwell of Georgia tonight at the Civic Centre.

The bout is one of five on the World Championship Wrestling pro card starting at 8 p.m.

Just under 5,000 fans attended the last Ottawa card April 30, but they were unable to see Bravo in action after he was told of his suspension — for missing a previous match in Toronto — while in the ring.

Organizers expect a crowd of about 7,000 tonight, when Verne Gagne and his son Greg taken on Nick Bockwinkle and Bobby Heenan in the tag-team, two-fall final bout.

Another match pits Mad Dog Vachon against Bobby the Brain, and Steve Osmonski meets Jesse "The Body" Venturi.

The 'official' story as it was reported in the newspaper was that Bravo had originally been suspended by Ontario Athletic Commission Chairman Jim Vipond for being an 'immature and irresponsible person' after no showing for Tunney. A quote by Tunney in the same article said that he 'had no concerns if he's (Bravo) allowed to wrestle in Ontario again, but he'll never wrestle for me again.'

As in other sports, never say never. Bravo would return for Tunney a few years later in 1982. Meanwhile not long after that first AWA Ottawa show in 1980, the ban ended up being lifted with Bravo in for the next card to wrestle Blackwell. Bravo would continue to wrestle for the AWA and Quebec based International Wrestling as Canadian champion as well as for George Cannon's Superstars of Wrestling based at that time in Windsor, ON. He was later called the WWF Canadian champion so was busy in that role after departing Toronto.

In answer to Bravo leaving the area, the office announced that there would be a one-night tournament to decide the next Canadian champion. Entrants were to include Angelo Mosca and Gene Kiniski, and once again Whipper Watson would present the title belt to the eventual winner.

When it was officially announced, the lineup included Mosca, Kiniski, and a substantial entrant list including Steamboat, Patera, Snuka, Valentine, as well as Pedro Morales and Mad Dog Vachon. Robertson would defeat Patera and Kiniski to earn his spot in the final. He pinned former champ Greg Valentine to become the new Canadian champion. ◆

Mid Atlantic Connection: Frank Tunney & Jim Crockett, Sr.

During the time of what we refer to as 'the Mid Atlantic era' in Toronto, promoter Frank Tunney was working with Jim Crockett, Jr. He had taken over the company (Jim Crockett Promotions) from his father Jim Crockett Sr. who had died in 1973. Frank & Jim, Sr. went way back in wrestling history and a look at the two men would note some parallels long before the two territories teamed up in 1978.

• Jim Sr. was born in 1909. Frank in 1912. They both started careers in pro-wrestling in the 1930s. Tunney took over the Toronto promotion in 1939 (in the office 1931-32) while Crockett started promoting wrestling as early as 1932.

• Neither had been wrestlers of note before turning to promoting as many had been in those days. Jim Sr. promoted various entertainment and sporting events (concerts, globetrotters basketball, fishing tournaments, etc.) as well as wrestling. Frank had a business diploma and some aspirations of being a sports writer before he chanced into the Toronto office - and loved it.

• Frank served as President (1960) and Vice President (1957-1959) of the National Wrestling Alliance (NWA). Jim Sr. served as Vice President (1970) and at times Chief Lieutenant for the NWA. Jim Crockett, Jr. also served as a President (1980-1982, 1985-1986) and a Vice President (1976). Both Frank and Jim Sr. were close with long time NWA President Sam Muchnick and were seen as calming and secure influences within the often troubled wrestling business. Neither was in at the start of the NWA. Frank had joined in its second year 1949 while Jim, Sr. joined in 1952, but both territories were often referred to as cornerstones of the NWA. Frank's nephew Jack Tunney would also be a President - - of the WWF (1984-1995).

• Family was important to both men. They married within two years of each other (Jim Sr-Elizabeth in 1935. Frank-Edna in 1937) and their families would be notably involved in both offices. Jim Sr. worked closely with his son in-law John Ringley, and delegated many responsibilities to all three of his sons, Jim, Jr., David, and Jackie. Jim, Jr. took over the company after Ringley left in 1974. Jim, Sr.'s daughter Frances worked on the baseball side of the family business.

• Frank had originally taken over the Toronto office with his older brother John who passed away suddenly in 1940. John's son John Jr. (Jack) would join his uncle Frank in the early 1950's and eventually took over after Frank's death in 1983. Frank's son Eddie (accounting) had also worked in the back office before officially joining cousin Jack to move the territory forward after Frank had passed on.

• They both also had Memorial Tag Team Tournaments held in their honor. In the South, there were three Jim Crockett, Sr. Memorial Cup Tag Team Tournaments (1986-1988), while up here they held a Frank Tunney Memorial Tag Tournament in 1987.

• Both Frank and Jim, Sr. were well respected members of the NWA as well as by the wrestlers and others who worked for them. I have never heard or read a bad word about either of them. Quite a feat for over 80 years combined in the world of pro-wrestling. ◆

CHAPTER SIX
The Title Years II: Robertson • Sheik • Mosca

The 1979 Tournament
Dewey Robertson: Local Hero

Dewey Robertson had debuted in Toronto in 1967 as the latest protege of Whipper Watson. He had always been a clean cut scientific star who had only partly lived up to his star billing since those early days. He had seen some success in the U.S. holding various tag titles while back at home he had formed a popular team with Billy Red Lyons known as 'The Crusaders.'

During the Crusader's run with our International Tag Titles (active since 1961 but brought back in 1974 to 1977), he ran a gym in Burlington just West of Toronto, and had since settled back into the local scene with an all Canadian look. Born in Hamilton, ON just outside of Toronto, he would become the first home-grown Canadian champion.

The tournament on September 9 to decide the new champion had been stacked with many stars, most from the Mid-Atlantic circuit and known to fans.

Mad Dog Vachon of course was well known to the fans but he hadn't wrestled in Toronto since 1973. He came in for a one-off during a busy schedule in the AWA, as did Lord Alfred Hayes. Former WWWF champ Pedro Morales had appeared on a few shows in the area but only once at MLG. He was at that time working regularly in the Mid-Atlantic area and would wrestle here a number of times into mid-1980. Greg Valentine was in the middle of a 9-month stint with the WWWF, having challenged Bob Backlund for his title on two MSG shows earlier in the year. Brute Bernard had once wrestled WWWF champion Bruno Sammartino at the Gardens (1976) and had settled in as a low-mid card guy. He had wrestled on the Dara Singh World Cup Wrestling show in Toronto at Varsity Arena just a few weeks prior.

With Vachon, Morales, and Gene Kiniski, there were three former big fed champs competing, as well as a few of the best young stars. Alongside Toronto regular Angelo Mosca, the tourney was filled out with Ricky Steamboat, Jimmy Snuka, Ken Patera, and Jay Youngblood, who were all starring in Mid-Atlantic.

As with many pro wrestling tournaments, the way they bracketed meant there would have to be some non-finishes or byes. Robertson would earn a bye after his second round win over Kiniski while Greg Valentine was to meet Ricky Steamboat in the semi-final but Steamboat had been injured in his previous bout with Snuka.

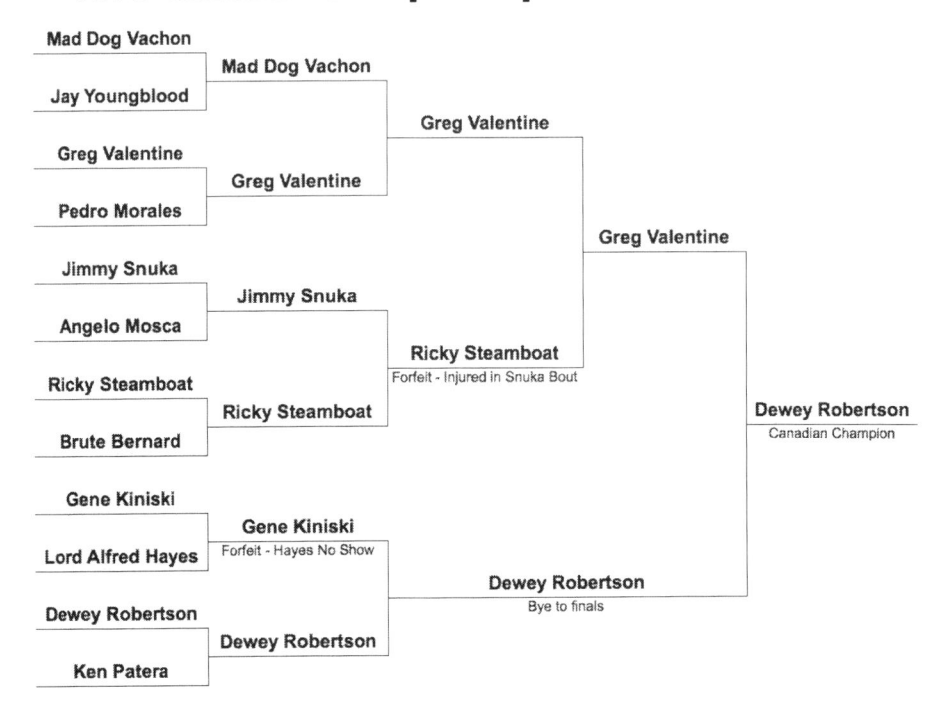

1979 Canadian Championship Tournament Results

```
Mad Dog Vachon ─┐
                ├─ Mad Dog Vachon ─┐
Jay Youngblood ─┘                  │
                                   ├─ Greg Valentine ─┐
Greg Valentine ─┐                  │                  │
                ├─ Greg Valentine ─┘                  │
Pedro Morales ──┘                                     │
                                                      ├─ Greg Valentine ─┐
Jimmy Snuka ────┐                                     │                  │
                ├─ Jimmy Snuka ───┐                   │                  │
Angelo Mosca ───┘                 │                   │                  │
                                  ├─ Ricky Steamboat ─┘                  │
Ricky Steamboat ┐                 │  Forfeit - Injured in Snuka Bout     │
                ├─ Ricky Steamboat┘                                      ├─ Dewey Robertson
Brute Bernard ──┘                                                        │  Canadian Champion
                                                                         │
Gene Kiniski ───┐                                                        │
                ├─ Gene Kiniski ──┐                                      │
Lord Alfred Hayes┘  Forfeit - Hayes No Show                              │
                                  ├─ Dewey Robertson ───────────────────┘
Dewey Robertson ┐                 │  Bye to finals
                ├─ Dewey Robertson┘
Ken Patera ─────┘
```

Our hometown boy Robertson would look unbeatable with wins over Patera, Kiniski, and Valentine all in one night to start his reign with the title. His former mentor Whipper Watson was on hand to present the title belt once again. Years later when Dewey wrote a biography "Bang Your Head: The Real Story of the Missing Link" he would mention that moment of Whipper handing him the title belt as a career highlight.

For his first bout here after winning the tournament, he would be tested by another champion. Once again, AWA World Title holder Nick Bockwinkel would come in to face our Canadian champ. This time however, only the Canadian Title was on the line. Robertson stunned everyone by making Bockwinkel submit to his figure four leglock. As it had done previously with Bravo, Robertson's status was elevated. They even covered it in a 'Wrestler' magazine in a story entitled 'Nick Bockwinkel's last hurrah?'

As with Bravo before him, Robertson would head out on the busy Mid-Atlantic circuit. Dewey though would wrestle as a subtle heel type, sometimes called a 'tweener' similar to how the NWA champs would work against local stars. He would face Youngblood, Rick McGraw, Jim Brunzell, Tim Woods, and other good-guy types in the Carolinas and across the Mid-Atlantic territory.

Robertson would also form a bond with Buddy Rogers. The original 'Nature Boy' and former NWA and WWWF champion. Rogers had returned to wrestling as a heel manager and had a stable that included John Studd and Jimmy Snuka. They had a small angle with Rogers teaching Robertson the 'right way' to put on the figure-four. Of course Rogers had used that hold effectively many years before.

Again, in Dewey's bio years later, he claimed Rogers really did help him improve the use of the figure four.

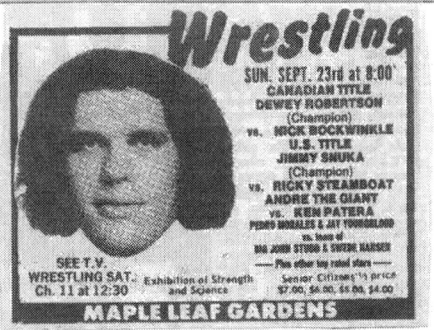

He would return to Toronto on October 15, 1979 to face Bockwinkel again. This time the AWA Title was on the line. Dewey had Bockwinkel tied up in the figure four as curfew was called and the bout was declared a draw.

Robertson would successfully defend against Ken Patera and then Jimmy Snuka. The 'Superfly' was the U.S. Title holder at the time and Dewey would look strong with a pin on his U.S. counterpart. The two would have a return match with both titles on the line - - U.S. and Canadian. Snuka's tag partner Ray Stevens interfered (Robertson win by DQ) leading to a short feud with Dewey teamed with Flair against Snuka and Stevens.

After a tag loss at MLG, the fans were pelting Stevens and Snuka with debris and Stevens lashed out from the ramp kicking a fan and sending him into an epileptic seizure. He also knocked out another fan who he claimed was attempting to get up on the ramp. Frank Tunney defended Stevens as being under attack and merely defending himself. The first fan pressed charges, with Stevens reciprocating, and both had to make a trip to Old City Hall in Toronto to answer them.

Robertson and Flair would also team at TV tapings in Guelph, while Dewey alone would see some high profile TV bouts including handicap bouts against two wrestlers at a time.

The Destroyer (Dick Beyer) had returned to Toronto in 1979 after a long absence. It had been 18 years since he had last wrestled here as Beyer

Robertson grabs wrestling crown

Dewey Robertson of Burlington won three consecutive matches in the elimination wrestling tournament last night at Maple Leaf Gardens and walked off with the Canadian heavyweight championship.

In the first round, Mad Dog Vachon defeated Jay Youngblood at 2:28 with a top spread. Greg Valentine pinned Pedro Morales at 13:47. Angelo Mosca was disqualified at 13:32 and Jimmy Snuka was declared the winner.

Ricky Steamboat pinned Brute Bernard at 7:17. Gene Kiniski was an automatic winner when his opponent Lord Alfred Hayes failed to appear due to plane connections.

Robertson won by a referee's decision over Ken Pantera.

In the second round Valentine used a top spread to defeat Vachon at 2:28. Steamboat beat Snuka at 15:37 with a reverse cradle. Robertson pinned Kiniski at 13:31.

In the semi-final event, Steamboat was unable to continue in the competition due to an injury in the Snuka match. Valentine was declared the winner of the semi-final leaving only Valentine and Robertson to battle for the championship.

Robertson defeated Valentine at 10:34 with a figure-four leg lock to win the crown.

(1961) and he had some immediate success upon his return including a WWF title shot (double count-out) vs. Backlund in early 1980. He had been offering opponents $1000 if they could break his own formidable version of the hold and insisted on being called 'the Original Intelligent Sensational' Destroyer. His impressive start had earned him a shot at Robertson and the Canadian Title in February of 1980 with Destroyer putting up his $1000 challenge against Dewey's title.

Destroyer would manage to apply the move several times but the champ would reverse it or reach the ropes on each attempt (not break it, so no $$$). Dewey held on to his title - barely - after getting caught in an airplane spin and using his feet to rebound off the top rope to fall on top of the challenger and get the pin. That card, featuring a Snuka-Flair U.S. Title bout as well as a violent Texas Street Fight between Blackjack

Mulligan and John Studd, would see an attendance of almost 17,000 fans, the highest in several years at MLG.

After defeating former champ Valentine by DQ (Valentine wouldn't break a chokehold) Dewey would suffer some ligament damage of his left arm in TV taping tag bout vs. Valentine and Stevens. He would be absent from Toronto but still worked a few bouts in the Carolinas in that time of recovery.

Once recovered, Dewey was set to get a shot at the NWA World Title held by Harley Race. This would be Race's 4th defense at MLG since he had won the title here defeating Terry Funk in February of 1977.

Dewey looked strong again, battering the NWA champ and reversing or escaping every hold Race tried. As curfew approached, Dewey clamped on the figure four just as time ran out. Officially a draw, but a big win for Dewey to hold his own with the world's best once again.

Great Hossein Arab: The Iron Sheik

On May 25, 1980 Dewey would lose the title to Great Hossein the Arab/The Iron Sheik. Hossein had made his name with a combination of great mat skills and strong conditioning which he sometimes displayed by swinging Persian Clubs. Hossein would dominate the bout and get the win after he 'loaded' his boot (he would kick the curled toe into the mat to 'load' it) and kicked Dewey in the throat leading to a pinfall victory.

The following day after the title win, Hossein teamed with Masked Superstar against former champ Robertson and his partner Angelo Mosca in Dundas, ON. The fans didn't know it yet, but Mosca would play a big part in the title scene moving forward.

Great Hossein, or Hossein the Arab/The Iron Sheik as he was sometimes referred to, was now a double title holder having won the prestigious Mid-Atlantic Heavyweight Title on May 11 in Charlotte, NC.

He would make his first defense in Niagara Falls against Flair ending in a wild double count-out. Flair was now a 'good guy' in the area after breaking from partner Greg Valentine. Hossein's first MLG bout would be a re-match against Robertson which he won convincingly by pinning the former champ. Again in Dundas the following day, he would team

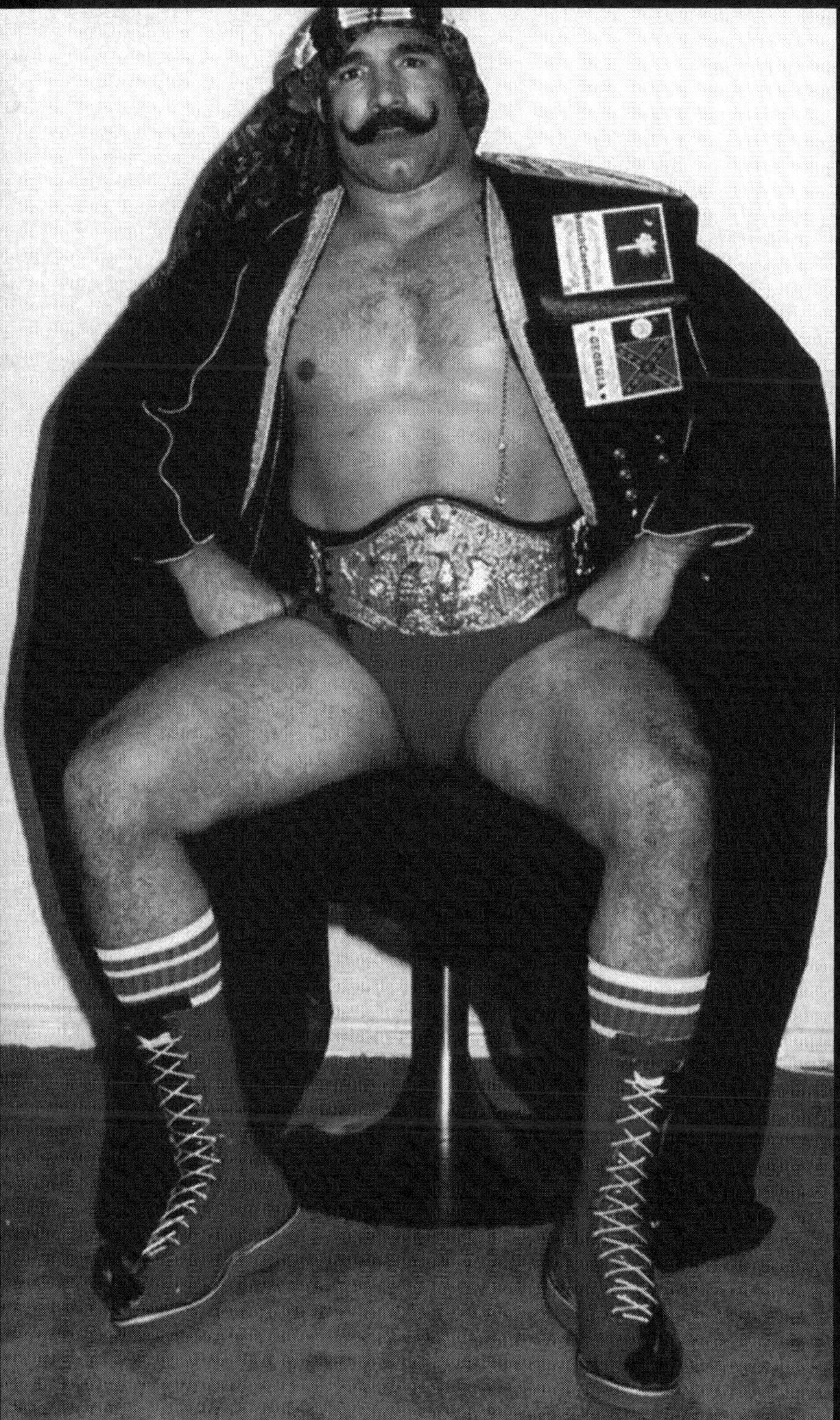

with Jimmy Snuka and Ray Stevens in a TV style 6-man tag against Dewey, Flair, and Mosca.

In a rematch with Dewey in June 1980, the former champ would take a page from the villain's playbook and attack Hossein at the bell ripping Hossein's robe and using a strip of it to choke the champion. After a flurry of illegal maneuvers and some timely distraction from manager Gene Anderson at ringside, Hossein would took the advantage. Dewey would manage to clamp on the figure-four but Hossein was able to make it to the ropes for a break. Hossein would eventually lock Dewey up in a small package cradle and earn the tough win.

At the end of the month, Hossein would face Angelo Mosca for the first time. Mosca would control the bout until both men went over the ropes to the floor. Manager Anderson handed his cane to his charge and after a beating with the cane and a run into the steel ring post, Mosca was soon laying on the floor covered in blood. Mosca finally made it back to the ring and took the upper hand attacking both Hossein and Anderson. He would refuse to break a sleeper-hold on Hossein and was promptly disqualified.

Hossein would have one more bout against Jay Youngblood in Niagara Falls before facing Mosca in a re-match at MLG on July 20. This time Mosca got the win and took the championship. The finish was disputed as Mosca had his feet on the ropes while pinning Hossein. Anderson claimed his charge was still the champ and disputes the loss, but to no avail.

The next day at a TV taping in Dundas, new champ Mosca teams with former champ Dewey & Ric Flair in a 6-man tag against Hossein, Valentine, and Swede Hansen.

It would be a short reign with Hossein taking the title back from Mosca on the very next MLG card. Then-fan and future wrestler Ron Hutchison remembers 'getting tipped off' by the Iron Sheik that he was going to win the title from Mosca:

> *Not a direct "tipoff" but in a more roundabout way when he posed the question to me asking, "How do you think the people would feel about me winning the title (off of Mosca)? Needless to say, I wondered if that was his way of telling me that he was*

going over for the title on that Sunday and, sure enough, when the final bell rang, Hossein the Arab, The Iron Sheik, Khosrow Vazari became the new Canadian Heavyweight Champion.

Hossein would give Dewey Robertson another re-match in October 1980, winning by disqualification and signalling the beginning of the end for Dewey's tenure in Toronto.

Next up was the increasingly popular Ric Flair getting another chance at the title, this time as the fan favorite. Flair would totally dominate the bout even escaping from Hossein's deadly camel clutch at one point. Flair would batter the champ from pillar to post leading Hossein to run from the ring to the safety of the dressing rooms. Flair would win the battle but not the belt.

Two weeks later, Mosca was trying for U.S. champ Greg Valentine's title and looked to have a win sewn up when he captured Valentine in a sleeper hold. From down the ramp came Hossein with one of his curled toe boots in hand. He proceeded to flatted Mosca with the boot getting Valentine disqualified.

After a defense in Buffalo against Masked Superstar the champ Hossein was back at MLG to face Mosca. This time Mosca got the best of the hated Hossein throwing him to the floor where he would stay while being counted out.

The re-match was set for a steel cage bout in Toronto on December 28, 1980. This time Mosca would get the win and take the title to begin his second reign. ◆

The Venues

Maple Leaf Gardens was the cornerstone for Toronto Wrestling for over 60 years (1931-1995). Tunney maintained a stranglehold on wrestling at the Gardens for the entire run, but there were other buildings that were an important part of the history. At times, too, Tunney's cards were relocated when the Gardens was under renovations or being used for a myriad of other purposes.

- In the early days at the turn of the century there were various locations you could watch wrestling in the city including Hanlan's Point, Riverdale Rink, and the Labor Temple.

- Arena Gardens/Mutual St. Arena was a regular spot and later became the main arena for Ivan Mickailoff when he started his weekly cards in 1929. It was located on Mutual St. in Toronto, near Massey Hall which had also hosted wrestling at times.

- Al 'Bunny' Dunlop ran Oakwood Stadium (Oakwood & St Clair) in the summer of 1947. Dunlop, a Tunney regular, would run with the blessing of Tunney and use some of the area regulars including Billy Stack and Joe Maich.

- In the summer 1949, Tunney promoted his first series of outdoor shows at East York Collegiate Memorial Stadium. Throughout the 1950s-1960s when MLG was not available on a wrestling night, they would often hold cards at East York Arena. Both were located in the Eastern part of the city where Whipper Watson, 'The Pride of East York,' resided.

• Maple Leaf Stadium, at the foot of Bathurst St. and home of the baseball Toronto Maple Leafs, was also used as a wrestling spot over the years. There was a show in the summer of 1959 and then a series of shows over consecutive summers from 1965-1967.

• In June 1971 Tunney ran a big show at Varsity Stadium with a reported 17,000 in attendance. The outdoor stadium on Bloor St. was the home of the University of Toronto sports teams and was packed for a battle between NWA champion Dory Funk Jr. and the Sheik, who was unbeaten in two years.

• George Cannon and his 'Superstars of Wrestling' ran the CNE Coliseum in June 1976 in an ill-fated attempt to go up against Tunney. The Coliseum was a small agricultural-use building on the Exhibition grounds, beside Exhibition Stadium.

• Exhibition Stadium, home of the Toronto Argos and the Toronto Blue Jays, would also host wrestling in the summers of 1977, 1983 (see Night of Champions, chapter 8), and in 1986 for 'The Big Event.'

• In 1979, the World Cup of Wrestling with Dara Singh held a card at Varsity Arena, an indoor facility next to Varsity Stadium.

• Smaller promotions and Indys including Dave McKigney would run some of the smaller arenas and halls around town including Scarboro, Ted Reeve, Lakeshore, and the Masonic Temple. Tunney also used Ted Reeve Arena for a card in 1957 (Opera in at MLG) and Scarboro arena in May 1963 for a Scarboro Youth Club benefit. ◆

CHAPTER SEVEN
Angelo Mosca: Bringing the Title Home

At the time Angelo Mosca first won the Canadian Title, he was a a vicious heel in the WWF and would appear there regularly while holding the strap. There would be no mention of Toronto while on WWF TV, but the magazines would have stories on him where they had observed the personality change depending on the location he wrestled. Mosca would reply with, "I wrestle the same way everywhere. The fans can decide to cheer or boo." He did and they would. He had previously been 'Ping Pong' Mosca in the AWA and was now back in the WWF gunning for Backlund's crown and prone to some serious fits of violence.

He would be managed there by Lou Albano and appear both on the WWF TV tapings and at the big shows around the Northeast. The Canadian Title belt stayed at home but he saw some success with several shots at WWF champ Bob Backlund at Madison Square Garden in NYC and in other cities on the circuit. He would also get shots at Intercontinental champion Pedro Morales, win a $10,000 Battle Royale in Landover, MD, and have a rare match against Andre The Giant at a TV taping in Hamburg, PA.

Mosca had mostly been an angry, hated heel for most of his time in Toronto. He had debuted here back in the Sheik era after starting in Ottawa in 1959 and was a regular during the previous AWA era (1977-78).

Mosca's first appearance of the new year in our area would be in Kitchener on January 10 for a tag bout with Blackjack Mulligan against Hossein and Bobby Duncum. The next night, wrestling returned to Maple Leaf Gardens with Mosca making his first title defense against former WWWF champion Ivan Koloff. Mosca would be disqualified and take the loss but keep the title.

Stranglehold

The Official NWA Toronto Magazine   *Sunday/February 22, 1981*

Big Angelo Mosca Goes To War With Hossian The Arab!

Will Their Hatred For One Another Ever End?...

ALL STAR ISSUE!
☆ ☆ ☆ ☆ ☆ ☆ ☆ ☆ ☆ ☆

*All New Action Photos
Exciting Stories To Read
Stranglehold Pin-Up
Plus Many Other Features!*

Stranglehold Magazine   Page 3

MOSCA vs SNUKA
Something's Gotta Give!

By Marty Slobin

MOSCA

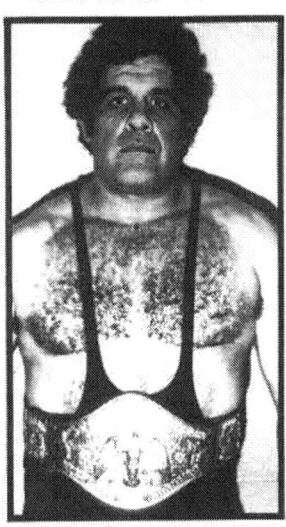

When *Jimmy Snuka* jumped *Angelo Mosca* after Mosca had put his arch-rival *The Great Hossian Arab* to sleep in the Maple Leaf Gardens main event, a new major vendetta had begun. The first match bewteen Mosca and Snuka was violent but inconclusive. Snuka won the match on a count-out, but Mosca retained his belt. Tonight there will be a clear-cut winner, and an obvious loser. At the end of tonight's encounter between the two, there will be an undisputed Canadian Champion.

"I may have to kill him," roared Mosca shortly after losing to Snuka via the count-out. *"Even though I battered that backstabber from the minute I jumped in the ring, he kept trying to steal my belt. I intend to make him bleed. If necessary, I may etch 'March 2nd' on to his body as well as his brain. Only when I feel that he has been punished enough, will I allow him to be pinned or put to sleep. This will be a long and bloody bout!"*

Angelo Mosca has the weapons to back up his words. In addition to the sleeper, Mosca is a master of the power-slam, the flying bodypress, and two devastating versions of the backbreaker. The ruthless Snuka has also perfected some incredible moves. In addition to the famous "Superfly Drop" from the top rope, Snuka can do damage with a flying clothesline, surfboard, temple rack, double-thrust, headbutt and rolling cradle.

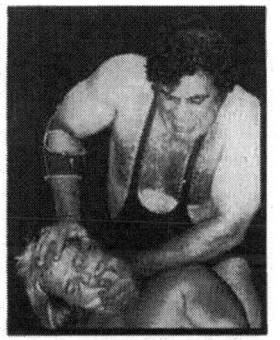

Mosca means business in the ring, especially when he's champion!

SNUKA

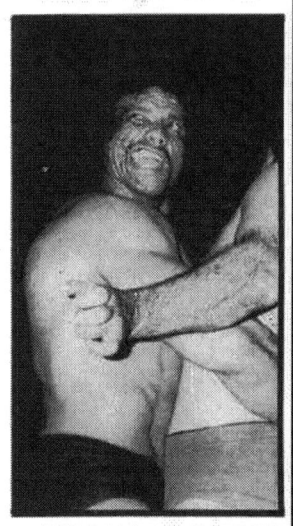

Snuka may even have come up with a new weapon with which he expects to win the Canadian Championship. He said, *"Although Mosca calls himself King Kong and attacks like some jungle animal, my speed, style and grace will distract and blind him to what he is really going to face. I have the ability to soar through the air like a beautiful bird while I reduce the gorilla to a bleeding heap of flesh. Remember, it was beauty that killed the beast!"* Then Snuka smiled enigmatically.

THE CANADIAN HEAVYWEIGHT TITLE

Defending the Canadian title in Florida (with Precious)

The next day at a TV taping in Brantford, Mosca took on former champ Hossein in a dark match which ended in a wild double disqualification.

Mosca was quick to establish himself as a tough as nails Canadian champion. With wins over Ivan Koloff, Bobby Duncum, and former champ Hossein, he would cement his status as the new fan-favorite of Maple Leaf Wrestling. He would also defend around the loop (mostly against Hossein) in Kingston, Brantford, Hamilton, London, Kitchener, and Niagara Falls as the MLW circuit went into full swing.

Next up was Jimmy Snuka. The feud started on the February 22 card when Mosca had Hossein in a sleeper hold and Snuka charged the ring to attack the champ much in the same way the feud with Hossein had been initiated.

Snuka won their first meeting, a violent brawl, when Mosca couldn't make the ten count back to the ring. Mosca kept the title. The re-match saw Mosca get a count-out win himself.

On the same card was Andre The Giant vs. Hulk Hogan in Hogan's debut match in Toronto. Andre and Hogan were taking their WWF feud on the road and this would mark Hogan's only appearance during the NWA days.

When ring announcer Norm Kimber made the announcement for the next show, Mosca was to be rewarded with an NWA title shot.

As with Bravo and Robertson before him, Mosca would challenge for the World title while Canadian champion. This time it was Harley Race and the NWA Title. This card was moved to a rare 1:30 PM start instead of the usual 7:30 PM, as the Maple Leafs were in a playoff series with the New York Islanders. If they went to a 4th game, it was scheduled for Sunday night at MLG. The Leafs were swept in three games but the show went on in the afternoon with both Mosca and Race being counted out after a tough brawl with very few wrestling holds.

Mosca was no stranger to celebrity. He had a long and noteworthy CFL (Canadian Football League) career in Hamilton just down the road from Toronto, and would later be inducted to the CFL Hall

Stranglehold

The Official Maple Leaf Wrestling Magazine — *Sunday/May 24, 1981*

MOSCA vs PIPER...

The Battle Of The Champions!

Photo/Brad McFarlin

Plus An All-Star Line-up On Tonight's Card!

of Fame (1986). His new-found popularity as the star of Toronto wrestling would attract some mainstream coverage which had been minimal in the recent past. All three Toronto dailies, The Globe, The Star, and The Sun would feature full page articles on the wrestling revival, with more coverage than had been seen in many years.

Big Ange was the star of several features both in and around Toronto and in other towns on the circuit. On the May 20 episode of the Global Network's "That's Life," one of the stories was 'a visit with Angelo Mosca.' On one visit to London for a card, he appeared on CFPL radio's "Sports Call" and people were calling in for 2 1/2 hours to talk to him. The Toronto Star also ran a full page feature looking at his wrestling and football careers with a photo from the Koloff bout in January.

After another re-match with Snuka under Lumberjack rules (Mosca win by pinfall), the champ would face U.S. champion Roddy Piper. Although Piper's title was not at stake, it had been billed as 'Battle of the Title Holders.' During their bout, Mosca would be attacked by Mr. Fuji. The ref had been knocked out and Mosca was on the verge of victory when Fuji stormed down the ramp and threw salt in Mosca's eyes enabling Piper to turn over on Mosca. The ref 'awoke' and saw Piper pinning Mosca and awarded him the victory. Former Canadian champ Dewey Robertson ran out and explained what had happened and the decision was overturned.

Mosca would win the revenge bout against Fuji and team with Ric Flair the next day at a TV taping in Dundas, ON, against Koloff and Tim Gerrard. They teamed again the next day in Oshawa where they beat Koloff and Fuji. In another TV bout, they teamed to beat Fuji and Piper. Both Mosca and Flair were now at the top of the fan's lists here. Both had initially wrestled in Toronto as heels but were now the 1-2 stars.

Mosca, as noted earlier, did not change his style while Canadian champion. He continued to cheat, use any and all illegal moves, and attack his opponents before, during, and after the bell. ◆

CHAPTER EIGHT
The Title Years III: Fuji • Studd • Slaughter

Mr. Fuji: A Blink of an Eye

On July 12 1981 Mr. Fuji finally defeated Mosca in a Texas Street fight to win the Canadian title. It would turn out to be the shortest of the title reigns with Mosca winning it back on the very next MLG card just two weeks later. There was a card in Buffalo, NY in between but the results are abbreviated so it's not clear if Fuji appeared or if the title had been defended. In all of the years since we still have not found a photo of Fuji wearing the Canadian Title belt.

Mosca would begin his third reign with the title first defeating Ray Stevens then Steven's tag partner Greg Valentine. Next up was a similar monster heel type who would prove to be an able adversary for Mosca.

John Studd: Big Man Champ

'Big' John Studd, fresh off his NWA title shot vs. Dusty Rhodes (August 1981) would beat Mosca for the Canadian Title on the next card held Sunday September 20. Of all the opponents for Mosca,

Studd would be one of the best matched. Both were big and strong and able to go toe to toe in the ring. There wasn't much in the way of wrestling holds with these two but they would have great slug-fests and bloody battles that were highlights of the era.

50th Anniversary Show: November 15, 1981

With the Studd vs. Mosca feud continuing, and Killer Kahn running roughshod over his opponents, a big card was set to commemorate 50 years of wrestling at MLG. The card to be held on November 15, 1981 was almost 50 years from the day November 19, 1931 when Jim Londos and Gino Garibaldi wrestled for the World championship at the then 7-day-old Gardens. Over 15,000 had attended that first event and over 16,000 would return to see the 50th Anniversary show.

In this era, there wasn't a lot of print devoted to pro wrestling in the city. In the 1940's and '50's wrestling would get a mention nearly every day in the sports section. By the 1980s there would a tidbit or two before the card, the ad, and then a small write-up or just the box score version of the card the next day. For this show, there was quite a bit of media prior to the card. All three of the daily papers would have features and the card was heavily promoted on TV and Radio.

It would prove to be one of the best cards of the year with the Gardens at an increased level of excitement to see a big NWA Title bout between the new champ Ric Flair (huge fan favorite here) and ex-champ Harley Race.

Wrestling
SUN. NOV. 15, 7:30 P.M.
TOMORROW 7:30 p.m.
WORLD TITLE
RIC (NATURE BOY) FLAIR
vs HARLEY RACE
ANDRE THE GIANT
vs KILLER KAHN
Canadian Title — 2 refs
ANGELO
(KING KONG) MOSCA
vs BIG JOHN STUDD
Also . . . Ron Bass, Von Hess, Johnny Weaver, Tony Parisi, Fulton, Davis etc.
SEE TV WRESTLING, Sat. CH. 11 @ 1 PM
Exhibition of Strength and Science
MAPLE LEAF GARDENS

Flair had been on a Buffalo card in October to face Ole Anderson in a strap bout, but this was to be his first title defense in Toronto. This was the second of six bouts these two had here over the NWA title between 1980 and 1984, and as usual was a great, non-stop battle. They would battle all over the ring, out to the ramp, and back again. They would exchange suplexes on the hard wood ramp and Race would cut himself open dropping his falling head-butt on the champ.

The fans, already huge Flair supporters, were solidly behind the new champ when Race appeared to get the pin. The crowd was stunned until ref John Laing came out and informed the acting ref Terry Yorkston that Race had pulled the trunks to win.

An argument ensued and Flair got behind Race, throwing him into the ropes and then a fast roll up and the win. Race was angry and attacked Mike Davis and Johnny Weaver, who had come into the ring to congratulate Flair. Race turned on Flair and gave him a piledriver leaving him flat on the mat. Race laid on a couple of his vicious knee drops by which time Weaver had picked up the NWA belt and swung it around in the air until Race retreated. The wrestlers then helped a bloody and beaten Flair down the ramp as the crowd went wild.

The card had already been a great one by the time of the main event. In a bout that was billed as a 'Super Grudge match', Andre the Giant was seeking revenge in the 'broken leg' angle with Killer Kahn. Andre, usually somewhat of a friendly giant, was enraged from the minute his large frame emerged from the tunnel and hit the ramp to the ring.

Andre looked to be (really!) killing Kahn when he pushed the referee out of the way and to the canvas. Earlier wrestlers from the card came out to help pull Kahn out of the ring to try and save him, Andre with his big paws reaching through the ropes at them. Both were eventually disqualified, but Andre had earned his revenge.

Our Canadian champion 'Big' John Studd was counted out in his bout against former champ Angelo Mosca. Big Ange was beating on Studd out on the floor when the champ, in a rather un-champion fashion, took off for the dressing room not to return.

'Outlaw' Ron Bass vs. Mike Miller, Johnny Weaver vs. Charlie Fulton, and Tony Parisi and Mike Davis against Doug Vines and Izzy Slapowitz rounded out the card.

Studd-Mosca Wars Continue

'Big Bad' Leroy Brown would get the first shot at new champ Studd on the next card. Brown had little wrestling skills but he had a big entrance on the ramp and seemed to be bouncing around for such a super heavyweight type. The fans here loved him. Studd got the win though, and it was announced that he would meet former champ Mosca on the first card of 1982, to be held on January 17.

The lineup for the first card of the New Year looked good. Two cage bouts! One between Johnny Weaver and Lord Alfred Hayes and another with Mosca getting a shot at Studd within the confines of the fenced in ring.

After a bloody Weaver-Hayes bout, they left the cage up for Studd and Mosca. The two would face down on the ramp as Mosca waited for Studd to climb the stairs. Mosca would attack and the bout was on. It ended with Studd pinning Mosca. It appeared that way anyway. Ref Terry Yorkston, inside the cage as was the case here, would get hit and in a daze (Yorkston played the semi-buffoon type well) awarded the victory to Mosca.

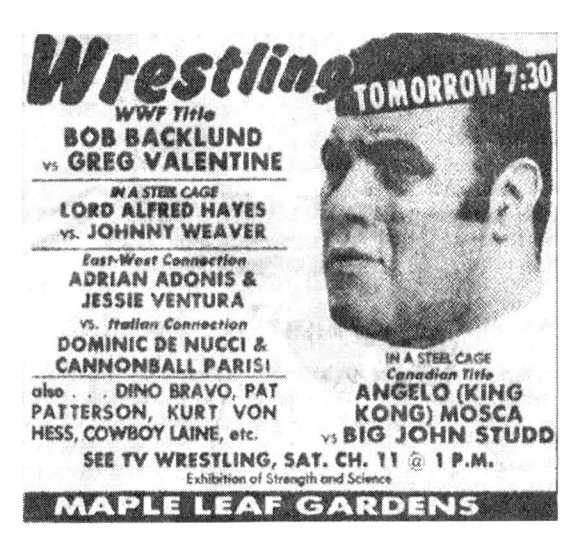

The fans went wild when Mosca grabbed the belt to celebrate but the celebration didn't last long with Studd viciously attacking the new champ. Weaver (bandaged up from his bloody cage bout) along with John Bonello would return to the cage to help Mosca, but both would take a beating from Studd before helping Mosca get the upper hand. A bloodied Studd emerged from the cage and took a whole lot of abuse from the fans on his way down the ramp. Mosca, bloody and beaten, emerged from the cage as the new champ to begin his fourth reign with the title.

In April, the feud between Canadian champ Mosca and Studd starts up again with Studd announcing he was bringing a mystery opponent to 'permanently maim the champ.' Studd had hyped it for the two weeks previous to the show. Fans were talking and many names were being brought up as to who could be the mystery opponent set to meet Mosca on the April 4, 1982 card.

One of those names was Andre the Giant. Andre was still a few years away from his first heel turn in North America, but at the time it seemed like a good idea. When the time came, it wasn't such a big name. When Norm Kimber announced.....Tarzan Tyler...the crowd was mildly disappointed to say the least.

Tyler was a ways past his prime by this point and of more importance, relatively unknown to the younger MLG crowd. He had appeared here sporadically from 1964-1978 and was a fine wrestler in his prime, but it was years removed from those days. Special ref Sonny Fargo had been assigned to officiate and the bout was generally a letdown since it had been so highly touted. Mosca didn't have much trouble in the end defending his title.

After the Mosca-Tyler card, Tunney set up a show to rival any in this era - here or anywhere. For the first time ever in Toronto, both the NWA and AWA World Titles would be defended on the same card. There had been a handful of WWWF/AWA double-title cards and one WWWF/NWA card, but never a NWA and AWA title match on the same card. The previous try was in 1979 but Harley Race had failed to make the card.

This one was set to see NWA champ Ric Flair face number one challenger Harley Race while AWA champ Nick Bockwinkel was to take on our Canadian champ Angelo Mosca.

A crowd of over 16,000 filled MLG to see the two champs successfully defend their titles. Flair and Race put on another classic, a bloody bout that saw action inside and outside the ring and on the ramp.

Bockwinkel was making his first appearance since 1979 and had a good bout with Mosca. Big Ange would batter the champ and looked to be on the verge of winning when Studd charged the ring and attacked Mosca. He and Bockwinkel laid a beating on Mosca until he was able to fight back and chase them from the ring. The official decision was a disqualification win for Mosca.

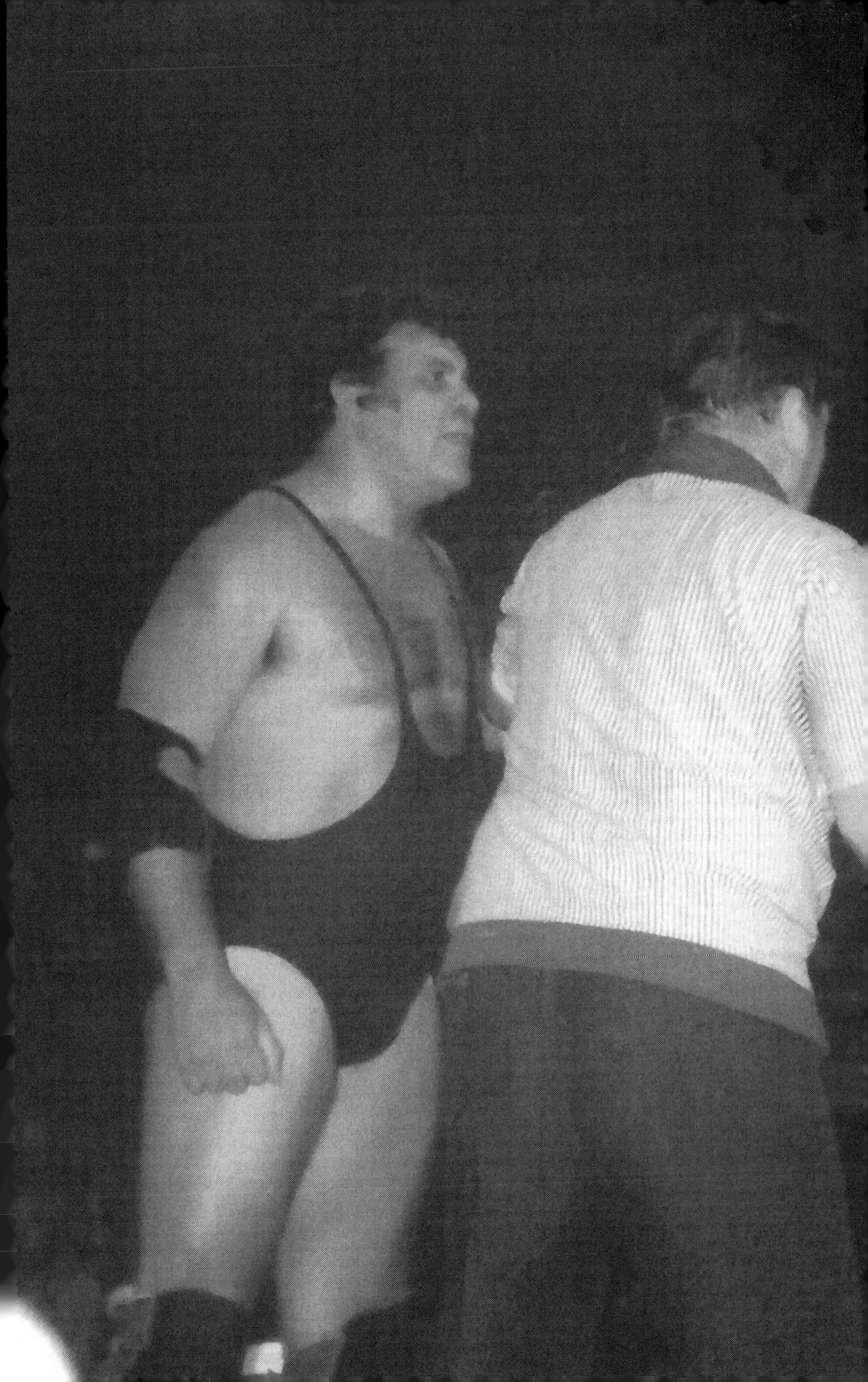

Angelo Mosca and John Studd face off on the ramp at Maple Leaf Gardens, January 17, 1982

Bockwinkel would return for the next MLG card to team with Studd against Mosca and Jake Roberts. Blackjack Mulligan Jr. was scheduled to team with Mosca but didn't appear. Roberts, who was fast becoming a favorite with his fast knee lift move, did double duty with a big disqualification win over U.S. champ Sgt. Slaughter earlier on the card.

Kiniski Returns

Another long time Toronto name would return in June to become Mosca's next challenger for the Canadian Title. Gene Kiniski, former NWA champ and long-time arch-enemy of Whipper Watson would

appear on the scene with his trademark growl and still a bit of gas left in the tank.

Next to Whipper, Kiniski was the only one to main event Maple Leaf Gardens in four different decades. He would complete that distinction by facing Mosca in the main on June 6, 1982. Unlike Tyler, Kiniski still had some name value here. He had been involved in the re-launch of the Canadian Title back in 1978 and his son Kelly had arrived a month earlier wrestling in the openers. This card saw both father and son in action, with Kelly teaming with Weaver to take on Sgt. Slaughter's recruits Don Kernodle & Jim Nelson.

Kiniski and Mosca was a tough affair with Mosca bloody by the end. Papa Gene could still go with the best of them and came off as a still-tough guy. His battles with Mosca and subsequent matches here and around the circuit and on TV were top notch and re-introduced him to the younger fans.

It was hard to believe that he had starred here 25 years earlier. Gene pushed the fact that he was still 'Canada's greatest athlete' (this was a few years before Mike Sharpe started using that) and was back in Toronto to regain his glory. In all, this would make over 250 appearances around Toronto since 1957, many of which were main events. He wouldn't succeed in taking Mosca's crown, but put up a good challenge for the champ.

The re-match against Mosca was a Texas Death match and Gene would go on the road appearing in Kingston vs. Jay Youngblood and again in St. Catharines for TV bouts against King Parsons and Pork Chop Cash. He would repeat a month later at MLG with a Lumberjack bout vs. Mosca and a road trip including Ottawa, ON for his last area appearance of this run.

Mosca would also face U.S. champ Sgt. Slaughter with only the U.S. Title at stake and finish out the year with a defense against the now heel Leroy Brown. A re-match with Brown in a steel cage bout was to be the main of the first card of 1983.

Mosca was spending more time away from Toronto with appearances throughout Florida, in addition to his WWF bouts. In Florida he would team with his Toronto arch-enemy Studd as well as his newest opponent here - Leroy Brown. Mosca would often be managed by J.J. Dillon and they would play up his Football background with specialty matches including a feud with the upcoming Butch/Bruce Reed.

In the WWF he would also team with another Toronto enemy: Sgt Slaughter. In those days the magazines were months behind so most fans didn't know what was going on in other areas. Some of us got the newsletters of the day including the excellent WWWN (World Wide Wrestling News) by Phillipe Zimmerman, which filled us in on all the happenings. We also got WWF TV here and had seen Mosca almost kill Pat Patterson with a water pitcher, among other indiscretions by the NY version of hated heel Mosca.

During his tours of Florida, Mosca would also defend the Canadian Title against Southern champion Ron Bass in a title vs. title bout, and team with Kevin Sullivan and Mark Lewin mostly against Blackjack Mulligan Sr. & Barry Windham (Blackjack Jr. here.) He would team with another Toronto opponent in Cowboy Bobby Duncum and they were billed as Global Tag champs for a bit making Mosca at the time a double title holder.

After the January 9 Toronto card where he beat Leroy Brown in the cage, Mosca would be absent until May returning to meet Bob Orton. Over the years, it's been suggested he was unhappy with the payoffs at the time, so he decided to work in Florida over Toronto. The payoffs at MLG for the main stars had long been determined by a percentage of the gate. With crowds down, those paydays would be reducing in the months to come.

Night of Champions/Return of the Champions: The Summer of 1983

When Frank Tunney passed away in May 1983, it was more than the end of an era. Frank was one of the wrestling world's longest serving promoters. Since taking over the promotional duties in 1939, Tunney had seen both ups and downs in the profession, but for much of the time, had been at the top of the game.

His long-time assistant and nephew John Tunney Jr. (Jack), who had been in a right-hand role since the 1960s, would push to maintain the promotion after Frank's death. Jack had been by his Uncle's side for many years, but was facing new challenges in changing times.

He would take a big risk and try to revitalize the territory with two big outdoor shows to be held in July 1983. Put on at Exhibition Stadium on July 10 and again on July 24, the cards could be considered 'Super-Shows.' Both were stacked with championship bouts and were a who's who of the stars of the day.

After a May bout vs. WWF Intercontinental champ Don Muraco, Canadian champ Angelo Mosca would return for the first outdoor show, dubbed 'Night of Champions', taking place July 10, 1983.

> **NEW PROMOTER JACK TUNNEY presents "THE EVENING OF CHAMPIONS" ON JULY 10 AT EXHIBITION STADIUM!!!**
>
> PROMOTER JACK TUNNEY

The Tunneys had put on wrestling cards at Exhibition Stadium before. In the summer of 1977, they ran three shows in the summer months in what would turn out be the end of the Sheik era. The shows were plagued by issues including an airline strike and the second of the three would mark the last appearance for the Tunney's by the Sheik.

Exhibition Stadium, on the shore of Lake Ontario, was known as 'The Mistake by the Lake' by the Toronto crowd. The long-time home for the CFL Argos and later the MLB Blue Jays, as well as a popular concert venue, the stages -or the rings -could be done in different configurations depending on the size of the event. Seating was over 43,000 for baseball.

A big issue due to the size of the stadium and the setup was that the ring was on the field, but with no ringside seats. Out in no-man's land. It ruined the usual atmosphere at the

Wrestling SUNDAY, JULY 10th, 8 PM
NIGHT OF CHAMPIONS

WORLD TITLE
RIC (Nature Boy) FLAIR
vs HARLEY RACE

NWA TV TITLE
HANDSOME JIMMY (Boogie-Woogie man)
vs THE GREAT KABUKI

CANADIAN TITLE | U.S. TITLE
ANGELO (King Kong) MOSCA | GREG VALENTINE
vs ONE MAN GANG | vs WAHOO McDANIELS

LADY'S WORLD TITLE | SPECIAL
THE FABULOUS MOOLAH | Dick Slater
vs PRINCESS VICTORIA | vs Big Joe LeDuc

WORLD TAG TEAM TITLE
RICKY STEAMBOAT & INDIAN JAY YOUNGBLOOD
vs DORY FUNK JR. & JAKE THE SNAKE ROBERTS

PLUS 3 MORE TAG TEAM BOUTS

Championship prices $15.00, $12.00, $10.00 & $7.00
Advance tickets available Maple Leaf Gardens 12 to 6 daily Info 977-1093

SEE TV WRESTLING SAT. CH. 11 AT 1 PM   EXHIBITION OF STRENGTH and SCIENCE
EXHIBITION STADIUM

bouts. At Maple Leaf Gardens, you could be up in the red seats about halfway up and it still felt like you were over the ring when the lights went out.

Mosca defended the title against One Man Gang in a bout that was all brawl before Mosca won with a pin. The program proclaimed it as the 'Battle of the Behemoths!'

In addition to the Canadian Title, the card was packed with five other title matches. In all, the card had nine bouts and would be deemed an unqualified success, despite different attendance figures reported (from 15-20,000).

Two weeks later, Jack ran the second card dubbed 'Return of the Champions.' Race and Flair would have a re-match with Johnny Weaver as special referee. Flair got into an altercation with Weaver and they came to blows despite Flair being a much loved fan favorite here.

Canadian champ Mosca would defend against new challenger Sgt. Slaughter. The hated Slaughter had been a regular here through much of the Mid-Atlantic era both on his own and with his charges Don Kernodle and Jim Nelson - The Privates.

As with Studd, the tough Drill Sergeant would prove to be an able foe for Mosca, and after a 20-minute brawl, took the title. It appeared that Slaughter had used a loaded arm brace to beat Mosca but the title change was declared official. We had a new champion.

While apparently not as successful as the first show ('Return' was a reported 14,000) the two Ex shows in the summer of 1983 would stand as two of the biggest cards of the era. It looked like things were turning around for Jack, but the next show at Maple Leaf Gardens dubbed 'Return to the Gardens' was sparsely attended. ◆

Sgt. Slaughter: U.S. Invasion

Slaughter would give Mosca a rematch in August 1983 in the first of 4 consecutive cards with Mosca trying to gain some measure of revenge as well as regain the title. They would have a no disqualification bout, a two referee bout, and finally a Lumberjack bout to settle the score. Mosca wins the Lumberjack bout but it is a

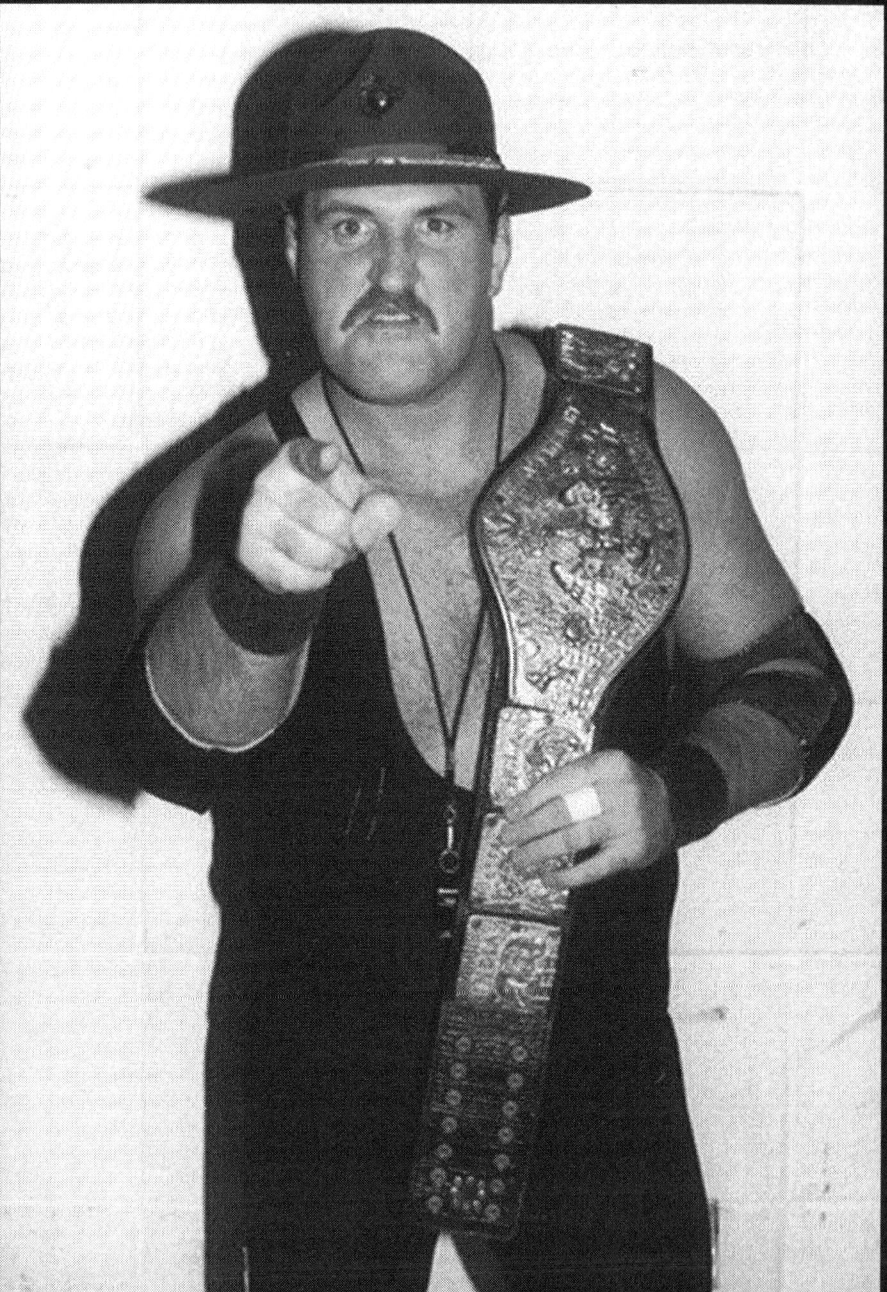

THE CANADIAN HEAVYWEIGHT TITLE

non-title bout. Slaughter is proving to be a tough champ in holding off the tenacious Mosca.

Slaughter's reign would last 6 months but other than Mosca his only other defense of the title would be against Blackjack Mulligan in October 1983. Slaughter would team with Kernodle against Mosca and Mulligan before facing Mosca again on the first card of 1984 losing by count-out. The re-match in a steel cage bout sees Mosca win the title to begin his 5th reign as Canadian Heavyweight champion.

Mosca would promptly disappear from Toronto to begin an extended stay down in Mid Atlantic alongside his debuting son Angelo Jr. Proud Dad Sr. would move his home down South and help Mosca Jr as he began his career.

With the Canadian Title mostly absent in early 1984 the North American Title would take its place for a time. That title was related to both the Calgary and Maritimes version and held by long time East coast and Stampede star Leo Burke.

By this time the quality of the cards in Toronto had dropped off with many of the Mid Atlantic 'A' stars no longer appearing on a regular basis. There were still many good wrestlers and able performers on the cards but the fans were used to a certain level of 'stars.'

As a result of the depleted cards Jack Tunney would begin using some of the Calgary based wrestlers including Bret Hart. He would wrestle here as Buddy 'Heartthrob' Hart as Barry Horowitz was using 'Bret Hart' at the time.

Meanwhile the absence of the Canadian Title went on for months. It was finally announced in April 1984 that Mosca had injured himself in the rematch back in January and that the title would be declared vacant. Once again there was to be a tournament to decide the new Canadian champion. ◆

Stranglehold

Back in the day the territories all had programs for the live events. They ran the gamut from handwritten to glossy professional works and Toronto was no different. Right from the 1930s, we had wrestling programs for both the early Mutual Street Arena cards and Maple Leaf Gardens. They were professionally produced and written by mainstream Toronto sports writers including Johnny Fitzgerald, Frank Ayerst, and long time Maple Leafs publicist Stan Obodiac.

Over the years they evolved though different sizes and formats. Everything from a 2-page folded in half to 50+ pages that included other sports that frequented Maple Leaf Gardens.

By the time of the Canadian Title debut in December 1978, there was no longer a program for the now twice-monthly MLG cards. In the summer of 1977 as the Sheik era closed out, they had issued a Maple Leaf Wrestling magazine/program. That was the last one for several years. They would have lineup sheets but the first program issued during the Mid-Atlantic era was a full two years after the debut of the Mid-Atlantic stars.

It was called Stranglehold and put together by Gary Kamansack under the Arena Magazine and Mancuso Publishing name. They were responsible for the Detroit area programs as well as the fabulous Wrestling Exchange magazine. They also did the programs for George Cannon's Superstars and for other areas as well. Slick feel with good (mostly) local photos with a lineup sheet as part of the program.

When Mancuso and Arena pulled out in 1981, it became a local production. The format stayed mostly the same although the look wasn't always as good. A lot of cutout photos and oversaturated ink but finally we had a program! They were only a buck or two as the era progressed, and have since become highly collectible.

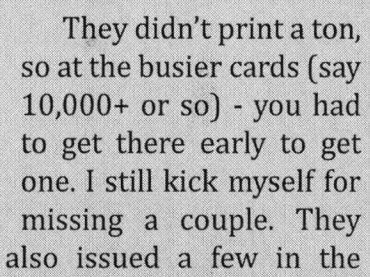

They didn't print a ton, so at the busier cards (say 10,000+ or so) - you had to get there early to get one. I still kick myself for missing a couple. They also issued a few in the circuit towns, a generic type with an inserted lineup sheet and at least one Photo Album right near the end in 1984.

Ric Flair, followed by Angelo Mosca and Jay Youngblood were the top three for being on the cover. Years later, I was fortunate to have Mosca autograph one for me. I handed him the pen and as he started to write, it promptly ran out of ink. He gave me that Mosca sneer but luckily another fan offered in a sharpie to complete the job.

The Strangleholds ran from 1981 right to the end of the NWA era in June 1984. They kept it for a time for the WWF shows before they moved to the popular and mostly generic WWF Magazine. ◆

WORLD TITLE MATCHES IN TORONTO
DURING THE MID-ATLANTIC ERA (OCTOBER 1978 - JUNE 1984)
(All matches at Toronto's Maple Leaf Gardens except where noted.)

NATIONAL WRESTLING ALLIANCE (NWA)

DATE	CHAMPION	CHALLENGER	RESULT
79/04/08	HARLEY RACE	RICKY STEAMBOAT	DRAW
80/04/13	HARLEY RACE	DEWEY ROBERTSON	DRAW
80/11/16	HARLEY RACE	RIC FLAIR	DOUBLE COUNTOUT
81/04/12	HARLEY RACE	ANGELO MOSCA	DOUBLE COUNTOUT
81/08/30	DUSTY RHODES	JOHN STUDD	RHODES WINS
81/11/15	RIC FLAIR	HARLEY RACE	FLAIR WINS
82/04/25	RIC FLAIR	HARLEY RACE	DOUBLE DQ
	DOUBLE WORLD TITLE NIGHT: AWA TITLE DEFENDED ON SAME SHOW		
82/06/27	RIC FLAIR	JACK BRISCO	FLAIR WINS
82/10/17	RIC FLAIR	DORY FUNK, JR.	FLAIR WINS
83/02/20	RIC FLAIR	TERRY FUNK	FLAIR WINS
83/03/27	RIC FLAIR	RODDY PIPER	FLAIR WINS
83/04/10	RIC FLAIR	RODDY PIPER	FLAIR WINS BY DQ
83/05/29	RIC FLAIR	GREG VALENTINE	FLAIR WINS
83/07/10	HARLEY RACE	RIC FLAIR	RACE WINS BY DQ
	MATCH TAKES PLACE AT EXHIBITION STADIUM IN TORONTO		
83/07/24	HARLEY RACE	RIC FLAIR	RACE WINS BY DQ
	MATCH TAKES PLACE AT EXHIBITION STADIUM IN TORONTO		
83/09/18	HARLEY RACE	MIKE ROTUNDO	RACE WINS
84/02/12	RIC FLAIR	HARLEY RACE	FLAIR WINS
84/05/27	RIC FLAIR	DICK SLATER	FLAIR WINS

AMERICAN WRESTLING ASSOCIATION (AWA)

DATE	CHAMPION	CHALLENGER	RESULT
79/01/14	NICK BOCKWINKEL	DINO BRAVO	BOCKWINKEL LOSS BY DQ
79/02/04	NICK BOCKWINKEL	TIGER JEET SINGH	BOCKWINKEL WINS BY DQ
79/03/04	NICK BOCKWINKEL	BILLY ROBINSON	BOCKWINKEL WIN
79/03/25	NICK BOCKWINKEL	BOB BACKLUND	DOUBLE COUNTOUT
	TITLE VS. TITLE (AWA VS. WWF) MATCH		
79/10/15	NICK BOCKWINKEL	DEWEY ROBERTSON	DRAW
82/04/25	NICK BOCKWINKEL	ANGELO MOSCA	BOCKWINKEL LOSS BY DQ
	DOUBLE WORLD TITLE NIGHT: NWA TITLE DEFENDED ON SAME SHOW		
82/04/26	NICK BOCKWINKEL	JAY YOUNGBLOOD	BOCKWINKEL WIN
	MATCH TAKES PLACE AT THE OTTAWA CIVIC CENTER, OTTAWA, ONTARIO		

WORLD TITLE MATCHES IN TORONTO
DURING THE MID-ATLANTIC ERA (OCTOBER 1978 - JUNE 1984)
(All matches at Toronto's Maple Leaf Gardens except where noted.)

WORLD WRESTLING FEDERATION (WWF)

DATE	CHAMPION	CHALLENGER	RESULT
78/10/22	BOB BACKLUND	IVAN KOLOFF	BACKLUND WINS
79/03/25	BOB BACKLUND	NICK BOCKWINKEL TITLE VS. TITLE (AWA VS. WWF) MATCH	DOUBLE COUNTOUT
79/05/13	BOB BACKLUND	MOOSE MOROWSKI	BACKLUND WINS
79/06/03	BOB BACKLUND	ERNIE LADD	BACKLUND WINS
79/06/24	BOB BACKLUND	GREG VALENTINE	BACKLUND WINS
79/07/15	BOB BACKLUND	RIC FLAIR	BACKLUND WINS COUNTOUT
79/08/19	BOB BACKLUND	KEN PATERA	BACKLUND WINS BY DQ
79/11/04	BOB BACKLUND	BARON VON RASCHKE	DOUBLE COUNTOUT
79/11/18	BOB BACKLUND	BARON VON RASCHKE	BACKLUND WINS
79/12/09	BOB BACKLUND	PAT PATTERSON	BACKLUND LOSS BY COUNTOUT
79/12/30	BOB BACKLUND	PAT PATTERSON	BACKLUND WINS
80/01/13	BOB BACKLUND	THE DESTROYER	DOUBLE COUNTOUT
82/01/17	BOB BACKLUND	GREG VALENTINE	BACKLUND WINS
82/07/11	BOB BACKLUND	JIMMY SNUKA	BACKLUND LOSS BY COUNTOUT
82/08/08	BOB BACKLUND	JIMMY SNUKA	BACKLUND WINS
82/10/03	BOB BACKLUND	BOB ORTON, JR.	BACKLUND WINS
82/10/31	BOB BACKLUND	BUDDY ROSE	BACKLUND LOSS BY DQ
82/12/12	BOB BACKLUND	BUDDY ROSE	BACKLUND WINS

CHAPTER NINE
The Title Years IV
Koloff • Mosca, Jr.

1984 Tournament & Ivan Koloff

With Angelo Mosca, Sr. absent and the Canadian Heavyweight Title declared vacant, it was time for another tournament.

The Tournament for the vacant Canadian Title was announced and would run on April 29, 1984. It was officially declared that Mosca, Sr. had been stripped of the title using the old NWA rule that the champion had to make a title defense within 60 days.

The tournament itself looked pretty good on paper, a mix of debuting names and some more well known to the fans.

The young favorites included top seeded Jay Youngblood and his younger brother Mark, who would be making his Toronto debut. Buddy (Bret) Hart had some big wins in Toronto and was in a feud

1984 Canadian Championship Tournament Results

```
Dick Slater ─┐
             ├─ Dick Slater ─┐
Johnny Weaver┘               │
                             ├─ Brian Adidas ─┐
Brian Adidas ─┐              │                │
              ├─ Brian Adidas┘                │
Tully Blanchard┘                              │
                                              ├─ Brian Adidas****─┐
Great Kabuki ─┐                               │                   │
              ├─ Great Kabuki ─┐              │                   │
Carlos Colon ─┘                │              │                   │
                               ├─ Angelo      │                   │
Angelo Mosca Jr. ─┐            │  Mosca, Jr. ─┘                   │
                  ├─ Angelo    │                                  │
Terry Kay ────────┘  Mosca Jr.─┘                                  │
                                                                  ├─ Ivan Koloff
Grappler #1 ─┐                                                    │  Canadian Champion
             ├─ Grappler #2* ─┐                                   │
Jay Youngblood┘               │                                   │
                              ├─ Double DQ                        │
Mark Youngblood─┐             │                                   │
                ├─ Mark       │                                   │
Grappler #2 ────┘  Youngblood─┘                                   │
                                                                  │
                                           ├─ Ivan Koloff ────────┘
Pez Whately ─┐                             │
             ├─ Pez Whatley ─┐             │
Jake Roberts─┘               │             │
                             ├─ Ivan Koloff┘
Ivan Koloff ─┐               │
             ├─ Ivan Koloff ─┘
Vinnie Valentino┘

Buddy Hart ─┐
            ├─ Buddy Hart** .....
Leo Burke ──┘
```

* Grappler #1 beat Youngblood, but was replaced surreptitiously by Grappler #2
** Burke injures Hart after the bout. Hart unable to continue.
*** After Mosca Jr.'s victory, Kabuki sprays mist in Junior's eyes. Mosca, Jr. unable to continue.
**** Adidas advances to finals when Mosca, Jr. unable to continue.

with Leo Burke over the North American Title. Brian Adidas, aka Adias (they did use the brand spelling here for a time), would also be making his Toronto debut, as was Puerto Rican mainstay and promoter Carlos Colon.

Colon had wrestled in the Toronto area on Dave McKigney's shows at Scarboro Arena and the other stops on the indy circuits back in the mid-1970s as Carlos Belafonte. He was one of those guys we only saw in the magazines up until then. He had been making some one-off type U.S. appearances around that same time.

Angelo Mosca, Jr., who was a late entrant, had been tearing up the Mid-Atlantic circuit and was the current holder of the prestigious Mid-Atlantic Heavyweight Title. He had regained that title from Ivan Koloff just a week earlier.

Tully Blanchard was another making his Toronto debut and was the current NWA TV champion. Jake Roberts was returning, this time as 'Snake Roberts', hated heel, and the tournament was filled out by some of the Toronto/Mid-Atlantic regulars at the time.

Ivan Koloff would persevere, winning over Vinnie Valentino, 'Pistol' Pez Whately, and finally Adidas to claim the championship and become the ninth title holder since its introduction six years before.

Angelo Mosca, Jr.

Junior, making his MLG debut in the tournament, would defeat Terry Kay and then face Kabuki in the quarter final. He would win the bout in just 38 seconds (always a couple of really short bouts in the tourney to fit all the matches), but Kabuki would spray his green mist and Junior would be out for the remainder of the tournament.

Two weeks later he would get the main event teamed with Senior against Koloff and Kabuki. They would appear together on the cover of the Stranglehold program and get the win. Prior to the bout, Junior told a reporter. "The best thing about wrestling is working with this guy (Sr.) right here." Senior replied, "I just hope I can pass on a few things to him."

The bout ends when Junior finally tags into to save his Dad from a beat down and pins Kabuki. The villains throw him out of the ring

Stranglehold

Official N.W.A. Wrestling Program SUNDAY/JUNE 10, 1984

IVAN KOLOFF DEFENDS CANADIAN CHAMPIONSHIP AGAINST ANGELO MOSCA JR.!!!

and go to work on Senior with Koloff's chain. Junior regains the ring and grabs the chain and chases the bad guys away to a huge roar from the crowd. The success would continue through the U.S. with Junior seeing success on the Southern circuit as well.

The two would appear on the same cards leading into a June 10 card at MLG which saw Junior get the win over Koloff and collect

Angelo Mosca, Jr. (2015)

the belt his father had previously worn. Only Senior was present at the next card and Junior's championship glory was to be short lived as it was announced a few days later that Jack Tunney was to work with the WWF. The title was retired (forgotten) with nary a defense by Junior.

With crowds waning in 1984, Jack Tunney and Eddie (Frank's son) Tunney decided to align with the WWF (publicly announced June 27) with the first card featuring only the new WWF stars on July 22, 1984. The title was just gone. It had come in with a roar but it went out with a whimper.

Junior would show up again in December of 1984, but with no mention of the title. Toronto was now under the WWF banner and he would appear on TV tapings briefly, while Senior was a short-lived announcer for the Hamilton/Brantford tapings. ◆

The Ramp!

It's one of the most memorable parts of Maple Leaf Wrestling for those who attended cards at Maple Leaf Gardens. It was the Ramp! An elevated walkway to the ring that was originally put in to protect the heels, specifically Nanjo Singh, from the wrath of the fans.

In 1948 when it was first used, the weekly cards were often brought to rioting by the heels of the day. Whipper Watson was in his prime and the star of the show. That made any of his opponent's public enemy #1. In particular the dreaded Nanjo Singh.

Nanjo and Whip had been feuding for years by 1948. Nanjo may have been the inspiration for The Sheik years later. A lot of biting, eye gouging, and foreign objects. It wasn't all an act either. The Sheik was Ed Farhat out of the ring, but Nanjo was still Nanjo out of the ring. Frank Tunney later noted that the only way he could get Singh to calm down was to threaten to call the cops. That's the only thing that scared him. He later went to prison (1958) for the murder of his wife in Philadelphia.

Whenever the fans got so enraged they tried to attack Nanjo he would escape under the ring. He would stay there until they could clear a track to the dressing rooms, usually with police and other wrestlers to form a protective line from the fans. The fans were used to this escape by then. 'Wild' Bill Longson had used it on many occasions in the early 1940s, also when battling the Whip. The fans loved Watson feverishly.

Even with the escape under the ring, Singh would still have to fight his way to the hallway that led to the dressing rooms, with fans attacking physically as well as throwing drinks, chairs, and anything else they could find. They would learn new tricks, too, including lighting papers on fire and throwing them under the ring to smoke him (Singh) out, 'like a porcupine.'

By 1948 Tunney had tried different measures to keep Nanjo both in the ring - and away from fans. The wire fence match, an early precursor to the cage match was used to varying degrees of success.

In May 1948, during one of those bouts, Singh was battering Watson into the ring post when a female fan jumped up and attacked

THE CANADIAN HEAVYWEIGHT TITLE

Big John Studd walks the ramp at Maple Leaf Gardens

Singh over the fence. The police rushed in to restrain her and Singh tossed Watson high and up out of the ring to crash down on the floor. Referee Cliff Worthy counted Whipper out while Nanjo strutted and taunted the fans from the ring.

As they were carrying Whipper out on a stretcher, Nanjo pointed and screamed "That's your champion!" The fans were enraged again. There were 11,000 in attendance and about 1,600 at ringside. Joe Perlove remarked in the Star the next day that while there were 1,600 at ringside "3000 tried to get at him." As the police and other wrestlers tried to shield him, he somehow made it safely to the back.

Anytime the fans got out of hand in those days, Tunney would get flak from the Ontario Athletic Commission. That may have led

Ric Flair battles Harley Race on the ramp at Maple Leaf Gardens.

to his decision to create a safer passage for Nanjo the next time the two met.

Right from the start it was called the ramp. It was described as an "elevated ramp from rinkside gate to ring apron which will be erected for the occasion. Nanjo will need it more than any of the others and it is questionable if even that will help him escape the wrath of the customers."

That first bout with the ramp in place went the same way. Whipper had dropkicked Singh off the apron to the floor where he was counted out. The fans gathered around him and Nanjo awoke in a hurry and jumped back in the ring to attack both Whipper and his manager Phil Lawson. Whipper took the upper hand while the fans crowded around the ring. Then Nanjo went through the ropes and "stepped out on that blankety-blank ramp and walked over the heads of the frothing populace."

Perlove opined that Tunney should have cared more about the fans that were unable to get their frustrations satisfied due to the easy exit by Singh on the ramp. Tunney was said to be quiet about the outcome until notified that Nanjo had split his head for 11 stitches upon whence he elicited a wide grin.

At any rate, it was a success. It had protected Singh from the fans, and as time went on there were other advantages to having the ramp there. Wrestlers could use the structure as part of the storyline (see slams, suplex's, etc.) and more importantly it created an entrance that the whole arena could see, no matter where you were seated at Maple Leaf Gardens. ◆

CHAPTER TEN
What's Become of the Belt?

So what became of the belt in the years following the switch to the WWF?

The belt ended up with former champion Ivan Koloff. Perhaps they were going to do another change from Mosca, Jr. to Koloff. When asked years later, Junior remembered winning the title (June 10, 1984) - but not leaving the dressing room with it.

In 1992, Koloff passed it to a well-known Southern wrestler who eventually sold it to a fan in 1997.

The fan made some repairs to both the cast and the leather and ended up passing it to belt-maker Dave Millican in 2000.

In November 2002, the belt finally came home when rabid fan and radio personality Griff Henderson (then of 99.9 MIX in Toronto) obtained the belt from Millican.

I was lucky to meet Griff around that time - and get a good look at the belt - as he was looking for pics of the belt and the champs wearing it. As a hometown fan, he was looking to fill in the story of our Canadian Heavyweight Title belt.

When he obtained the belt, the black leather strap had apparently been altered since the original days. As well in some pictures with Sgt. Slaughter in 1983, the leather appears to be of the reddish/brown hue that Mulko often used, not the original black. In later pics with Mosca in 1984, the strap is black again.

It was still black in 2002, though it's not clear how many times the strap may have changed. They used it as a weapon a lot and likely damaged the belt on numerous occasions. Mulko, still somewhat local, could be called upon to fix it.

Griff Henderson, aka Barry Hatchett (2003)

Another interesting change that was evident was at the end of the strap. It originally had a hole at the clasp end, perhaps to hang the belt on a dressing room peg. That was now another clasp in line on the strap when purchased in 2002.

It had also been gold re-plated including the main eagle that had been silver on the original. The fan that had obtained the belt in 1997 had once commented that the leather was 'tan' when he had originally obtained it so it further muddles it. It had seen some modifications since it had been retired back in 1978.

Griff would also have doubts about the authenticity of the belt as it was engraved after all - as the TWWA Heavyweight Wrestling Champion. He reached out to Angelo Mosca, Sr. who was less than congratulatory when he heard what the belt had cost long-time fan Griff. The still surly Mosca was also sure IT DID NOT say TWWA on it. That's when Griff contacted others to obtain some photographic evidence of the original 1978-1984 belt.

His whole story from 2003 is on Slam! Wrestling:

"Confessions of a Canadian Title Junkie"
http://slam.canoe.com/Slam/Wrestling/2003/09/24/201512.html

Griff headed for an East Coast tour, and finally in 2009, he passed the strap onto another lucky local fan who had been obsessed with title belts since he was a kid, Chris Kovachis.

Chris related his story to me on how he came to own the Canadian title. He still has the belt to this day and is a collector of original Mulko cast belts and owns several from which you can buy your own cast copy.

Thanks to Chris for sharing his story and contributing to this book. ◆

Keeper of the Belt
by Chris Kovachis

I was hooked the first time I saw Dino Bravo on Channel 3 come to the rescue of a bloody Gene Okerlund before Sailor White could tear his limbs off. On channel 11, I was flailing away at Mr. Fuji after he threw salt into King Kong's eyes as he stole the Canadian Heavyweight title from his grasp! Our title ... Canada's, title!

The 'holy grails' from my childhood were the 10 Lbs. of Gold NWA World title, and the Mulko created Canadian Heavyweight title.

The Mulko style belts were all around back in those days with U.S. champion Sgt. Slaughter wearing that gold in the shape of the USA! I was so interested in being part of this business and owning a real wrestling championship belt that even as a 13 year old kid, I created my own 'world wrestling league.' I would have my friends compete for my makeshift prize, which were my championship belts that I made from wooden style steak plates with sheet metal attached to an old belt.

Around 1995-96, I first caught sight of replicas being offered online. I couldn't believe my eyes as you could purchase an exact replica of the WCW World Title belt for only $150 US! Then a few years later, I added the 10 Lbs. of Gold to my collection as well.

I was later able to purchase my first Mulko-style real replica that was cast from Manny Fernandez's NWA World Tag team title belt.

Around the same time I had seen an ad in which a fan had posted on eBay about purchasing the Toronto Stranglehold programs. He related to me that he had in his possession the ring used Canadian Heavyweight title belt. Anxiously, I asked him if he would mind bringing the belt with him when he came to purchase my Stranglehold doubles, as I was a huge fan of that belt! I was able to see it, touch it, and take several pics with the 'holy grail' that day and we left as good acquaintances.

I left hoping that someday a ring used championship belt would grace my hands. One day.

Little did I realize that some 8-10 months later it happened in the form of another beautiful Mulko belt that was once held by Freddie Blassie: The Pacific Coast Heavyweight title belt.

I was the new owner of my first ring used championship belt. I must say, it is the most beautiful Mulko that I have ever seen in person and is still in immaculate shape for a title belt that's almost 50 years old!

Then in 2009, years later, I get contacted by the fan with the belt and he is asking if I would like to purchase his Canadian Heavyweight title belt. I agreed and I became the newest owner of the ring used Canadian Heavyweight title belt!

Seeing as now I was the owner of these prestigious title belts, and witnessing other belt makers replicating others, I decided to search for a local company that would be able to produce replicas of my title belts. I had hopes that some fans out there, like myself, loved these titles so much that they would like to own a replica of their own favourite belt.

I was fortunate enough to find a local caster where I was able to produce molds of the plates for the Canadian, the Blassie Pacific Coast, and the WWWF Tag title plates. In addition to those I am now able to also replicate the U.S. Heavyweight title, the NWA World Tag team title, and the WWWF World Titles; the Backlund/Graham/Sammartino, & Pedro versions. ◆

'King Kong' Mosca checking out the
Canadian Title belt

There is only one Canadian Title!
But you can get an exact cast replica

The replicas Chris makes are incredible!
For more info on how to obtain one of these belts
visit his Facebook page at

'MULKA CHAMPIONSHIP BELTS'
https://www.facebook.com/groups/526327670760211/

Maple Leaf Gardens, 2005,
now home to the Mattamy Centre.

CENTRE GARDENS

Epilogue

The story of the Canadian Title ends with the beginning of a new age in Toronto wrestling history. Most people describe it as 'Toronto selling to the WWF,' but that isn't accurate.

The new venture that Frank Tunney, Jim Crockett, Jr., and George Scott had started in December 1978 changed when Frank passed away in 1983. It went from the Tunneys owning 50% to only owning 33%. The three parties never agreed on the terms of a new partnership moving forward. Frank's son Eddie also took on a more prominent role alongside his cousin Jack as they tried to forge ahead after Frank's death.

By early 1984, many of the stars of the Mid-Atlantic were not appearing here as often as previously. Jack Tunney went to Calgary promoter Stu Hart for help. It was to be a win-win proposition as Toronto needed talent and Hart needed more dates for his wrestlers. Jack and Eddie needed a short term fix until they could get out of the deal with Crockett. It was similar to when Frank had used the AWA main stars to fill in after the Sheik era was done. The benefits of using Canadian talent were two-fold. There were no customs or border issues to deal with - and it didn't tip off Crockett about Jack's future plans.

Jack & Eddie may have been investigating a partnership with Vince K McMahon and WWF as early as January 1984. (Jack was in New York when Hogan won the title). They further negotiated a deal with McMahon around the time they attended the funeral for Vince's father in May 1984. Hamilton star George Scott, the third partner in the original 1978 Tunney/Crockett arrangement, was by then also working in an executive capacity with the WWF.

The new Maple Leaf Wrestling was formed in June 1984 during a meeting with McMahon, Eddie, and George Scott at Vince's house. The meeting took place at the time of the second-to-last NWA show at MLG (June 1984). The partners were now 50% Titan Sports (WWF), 33.33% Tunney Sports (50% Jack, 50% Eddie) and 16.66% George Scott. The deal was such that Tunney Sports would continue to run the business but only use WWF talent. McMahon and the WWF invested no money in the partnership.

Tunney Sports would also work for Vince in other areas outside of Ontario such as Buffalo and Detroit.

In 1987, Jack & Eddie would have a falling out with George Scott and he was excluded from the business.

While Jack became the on-air and acting 'President' of the WWF, it wasn't until November 1989 that he became the actual President of Titan Promotions Canada, Inc.

That same year McMahon told the Tunneys he was no longer going to use Maple Leaf Wrestling. He would use Titan Promotions Canada to operate the business and offered Jack the job as president of the Northern arm of Titan.

That same year Eddie Tunney sued both cousin Jack and Titan Sports after they left him out of a new deal. When Titan's lawyers looked at the suit, they advised Vince to settle right away. It included everything from trademarks (Eddie had trademarked the Wrestlemania name in

Canada) to the deposit cheque for the Skydome (for WM6) that came from Tunney Sports which Eddie had signed. No one seems to know the details of the settlement because Vince dealt directly with Eddie. The suit had asked for all the profits from Wrestlemania 6 both live gate and pay per view to go into a trust until it went to court. Vince and Eddie settled and the show went on here. That was the official end of the Toronto office.

Crockett also sued the Toronto office's holding company, 'Frank Tunney Sports Limited,' and settled for a reported $11,000. The way the partnership had been shut down was all above board with that money covering old shows.

As a result in the end, McMahon never paid a dime for the area. ◆

124

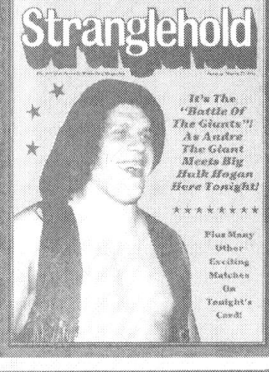

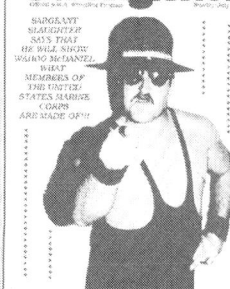

PHOTO INDEX & ACKNOWLEDGMENTS

PAGE	PHOTO	SOURCE
12	Frank Tunney	Photo that hung in the Hot Stove Lounge at MLG
15	Frank Tunney Lord Layton, Jerry Hiff	Roger Baker photo
16-17	Frank Tunney, Barry Lloyd Penhale	mapleleafwrestling.com collection
18	Frank Tunney, Gene Kiniski	Roger Baker photo
20-21	MLG crowd shot 1972	Roger Baker photo
34	Dino Bravo, Whipper Watson	Globe & Mail used with permission/license
37	Frank Tunney Belt Buckle	Shared by Tunney family
38	Alex Mulko	mapleleafwrestling.com collection
46	Dino Bravo	Jackie Crockett photo - used with permission
48	Dino Bravo	Griff Henderson collection
50	Dino Bravo, Tony Atlas	Jackie Crockett photo - used with permission
52	Dino Bravo, Greg Valentine	Chris Swisher collection - used with permission
53	Greg Valentine	Griff Henderson collection
54	Johnny Valentine, Gene Kiniski	Roger Baker photo
55	Greg Valentine, Dino Bravo	Griff Henderson collection
59	Dino Bravo	Griff Henderson collection
63	Dewey Robertson	mapleleafwrestling.com collection
66	Dewey Robertson	Jackie Crockett photo - used with permission
69	Great Hossein Arab	Griff Henderson collection
72	Maple Leaf Gardens	mapleleafwrestling.com collection
75	Angelo Mosca	Griff Henderson collection
78	Angelo Mosca, Precious	Pete Lederburg collection - used with permission
83	John Studd	Griff Henderson collection
88-89	Angelo Mosca, John Studd	mapleleafwrestling.com collection
96	Sgt Slaughter	Griff Henderson collection
101	NWA World Title Belt	Dick Bourne photo / Mid-Atlantic Gateway
106	Angelo Mosca Jr	Griff Henderson collection
109	John Studd	Griff Henderson collection
110	Ric Flair, Harley Race	mapleleafwrestling.com collection
113	Griff Henderson	Griff Henderson collection
115	Chris Kovachis	Chris Kovachis collection
117	Angelo Mosca	Chris Kovachis collection
118-119	Maple Leaf Gardens	mapleleafwrestling.com collection
All Canadian Title belt photos		Chris Kovachis collection
Some images from nostalgia of the day.		mapleleafwrestling.com collection